EIGHT TEN TO CHARING CROSS

Delusions and Daydreams
of a 1950s Teenager

Jean Hendy-Harris

Copyright 2017 Jean Hendy-Harris
Print edition

Smashwords Edition 2014

All rights reserved. No part of this book may be used or reproduced in any manner whatsoever including Internet usage, without written permission of the author.

Ebook formatting by Maureen Cutajar
www.gopublished.com

A continuation of the autobiography started in

CHALK PITS AND CHERRY STONES

ISBN-13: 978-1978107472
ISBN-10: 1978107471

Autobiography, London, 1950s, teenager, music business

Phone Shy

I was about to start working for a living! Halfway through the first school term of 1956 I had been interviewed and accepted for a job as a junior shorthand typist for a music publishing company in Charing Cross Road. It was all very exciting but there were intervening weeks of schoolgirl-hood still to navigate and someone who is about to turn sixteen resents being reprimanded for lapses in dress code or cheekiness to a prefect. The days passed agonisingly slowly.

We went on an Easter holiday break that year to our favourite caravan and chalet site. Our family of three, together with `Old Nan' my grandmother, several aunts, a number of cousins who seemed totally grown up and two who were still younger than me, Ann and `Little Violet' who were twelve and ten respectively. My mother had chosen the hire of a caravan over that of a chalet because it was the cheaper option and conveniently situated adjacent to the site facilities but the remainder of the family spread themselves through three or four of the cliff-top chalets, two of which had views over the grey waters of The Swale, the characterless strip of water that separates North Kent from the Isle of Sheppey. The Swale today occupies a special place ecologically and is both a National Nature Reserve and a Special Protection Area boasting significant plant species such as Eel Grass, White Seakale and Golden Samphire. Certain uncommon migrant butterflies and moths dally between and above the plant life such as the Essex Emerald, the Ground Lackey and the Clouded Yellow Butterfly. Day visitors with notebooks and binoculars speak respectfully of rare Hawk Moths and will tell you that since 1968 it has been a Site of Special Scientific Interest. Fifty years ago, however, it was little more than host to the run-down caravan site which we frequented because it was, according to my mother, cheap and cheerful. She enjoyed Swalecliffe but Old Nan said it was a `one-eyed dead-alive' place and enough to drive anyone to drink. Not that she needed much driving.

I always found the holidays unbearable and prayed for them to pass quickly. One of the reasons was because they were boring to the point of being mind-numbingly tedious and the other was because older male cousins were apt to use these family occasions as opportunities to carry out minor acts of sexual assault on me. The Easter holiday break by The Swale was no different. I assuaged the anger and relieved the boredom by systematically bullying my brother and two younger cousins.

`Today,' I announced on the first Saturday when the trip into Whitstable to the public bar at Pearson's Oyster House had been postponed until the following day for some reason, `Today we are only going to speak French. We will not speak a word of English.'

Ann looked at me in some alarm. `But I can't speak French.'

Bernard and Little Violet exchanged glances and said together that they didn't speak French either.

I felt exasperated. 'Well neither do I. We're going to make it up. Nobody will realise that it's not French as long as we don't stop speaking. And we're going to choose French names. I'm going to be Dominique.'

Dominique was to be nearly sixteen years old, like me, and on an Easter break holiday from Paris with her younger siblings and the four of us would wander through Whitstable the next day as affluent French visitors who had flown in, minus parents or guardians, just for a few days to catch a glimpse of how life was lived in rural Kent. We would be booked into the Jolly Sailor Guest House. It was all going to be vaguely reminiscent of the best of Enid Blyton whom I had not yet entirely relinquished.

Little Violet said she would like to be called Sharon in that case and I pointed out so forcibly that Sharon was a totally unsuitable name for a French visitor that she began to cry and said she didn't really want to play at all because it was a stupid game.

'You can be Suzette,' I tried to sound kinder in case she took it into her head to run complaining to one of the aunts. 'Suzette's a really lovely name – and Ann can be Marie and Bernard can be Jean-Paul.'

Bernard looked suspicious, 'Is that a boy's name?' adding, ' I don't want to be Wendy any more.'

When he was younger he seemed not to mind being Wendy but had become more rebellious with age. We had wandered along the track behind the camp site to the bridge over the stream where there were always dragonflies hovering above the water. This was where I had been taken for the purpose of sexual molestation on several occasions the previous summer.

'We'll start speaking French now,' I said, 'I don't want to hear another word of English.'

But infuriatingly none of them would co-operate, not even Ann when I threatened to hold her upside down by her feet from the middle of the bridge. Later she told her older sister Margaret who righteously defended her and said it was a good thing I'd given up the idea of becoming a nun because that kind of behaviour would never be tolerated within convent walls.

But I had not totally given up the idea and spent the next few days in an agony of indecision. I was immersed in my wavering thoughts and idly observing a Marsh Harrier arc the sky when one of the boys, recently jilted by a fiancée called Eileen, came across me on the cliff path and suggested a walk to the dragonfly bridge. When I told him I was too busy at present deciding whether to become a nun or not, he hastily retraced his steps back to the chalet without a word and avoided me for the remainder of the holiday. On examining my reasons for opting for the religious life carefully I had to admit that the most compelling incentive was the habit. I thought it would rather become me. Deborah Kerr, or was it Audrey Hepburn? looked sensational in hers in a film at The Majestic last winter. Quite apart from that, the garment disguised a multitude of body shapes and I had not been growing more slender as I progressed into my teens. Back at school I conveyed my indecisions to the woman in the office who nodded without interest. The next day the

Deputy Headmistress was helpful and kindly suggested that she should enquire whether I could put the job in the Copyright Department of Francis, Day & Hunter on hold for the time being whilst I thought things through. My last days as a schoolgirl were spent tossing first one and then another scenario around in my head. I could come to no sensible conclusion and in the end decided to flip a coin, then flip twice more – the best of three! The priority after all was to cease to be a schoolgirl.

So yes, I would indeed enter the religious life. I discussed the decision at length with Sister Camilla my favourite nun from the school my brother now attended. She prayed for me constantly she said and she must have done because The Sisters of Mercy, founded in Dublin in eighteen thirty one, agreed to give me a go. Their original London convent had been in Bermondsey, established as early as eighteen forty and twenty years later they sent the first Sisters to Gravesend to carry out their Mission. Reverend Mother explained to me that they were 'Apostolic women who had dedicated their lives to God by vows of poverty, chastity and obedience as well as service to the poor.' She went on to enumerate the wide ranging social needs they concerned themselves with.

'Our aim is to alleviate suffering,' she said sternly, 'We make a difference! Are you sure you want to do the same?'

I nodded at once and she went on to talk about the number of years it was going to take me to become a fully-fledged member of the community, explaining the various steps along the way and the important difference between temporary vows and final vows. It was clear there was going to be no short cut to the top.

When Nellie, my mother, finally confirmed the news of my chosen career path to the rest of the family there was a great deal of shock and disbelief and Old Nan said she'd never heard of anything more bleeding daft in all her born days and furthermore I gave her the pip.

'Well what was all them typing classes about then?' demanded Aunt Maggie, looking mystified, 'Cos them nuns don't type do they?'

'You'll be an old maid,' my cousin Patsy told me, 'And you won't like that very much.'

It was generally agreed that I would probably 'grow out of it'.

Over the following turbulent few months I learned that the life of a nun was not all it was cracked up to be and seemed to involve a lot of housework and preparing of vegetables for nourishing soups and once the fact that I could type was revealed, a lot of typing as well. A girl of about my own age called Bridget O'Brien had entered in the same week as myself and I asked her if she thought we had made the right choice hoping that she would break down in tears and confess her own doubts. But instead she smiled and clasped her hands together and said she was happier than she had ever been in her life which was a bit disappointing. But in the end it was easier to escape than I imagined because it transpired that I was not totally suitable and I had been wrong about having a Calling. It also had something to do with leaving the premises without permission to make Saturday afternoon trips to the cinema and encouraging Bridget to go with me, which on one occasion she did. In the end Bridget was allowed to stay but it was suggested that I might like to leave and once I stopped feeling offended it was a relief. I had rather hoped to rise to the position of Mother Superior in the shortest space of time possible because at the age of almost sixteen it definitely appeared to me that the local Mercy Sisters and indeed the entire Religious Order was in need of an organisational overhaul. Common sense dictated that it would be prudent to begin the task from a position of authority but it was clearly not to be. The prevailing Reverend Mother had to my mind seemed doggedly determined to keep me at the very bottom of the pecking order for as long as possible. Eventually, following the discovery of being caught out of bounds for the second time, she told me that I had been quite mistaken in thinking I had a Calling for the religious life. Possibly, she suggested, her hand hovering over the telephone in front of her, my Calling should have been more properly directed into nursing. It was easy to make that particular mistake she said, and it certainly wasn't the first time it had happened. Furthermore the local hospital would be very glad to have me. She decisively began to dial the number.

The hospital said they would be pleased to have me and the transformation from trainee nun to trainee nurse took place with startling rapidity. There was little time to tell my mother and barely time for her to board the Crayford bound bus to inform the family.

'When's she going to make up her bleeding mind and start bringing a pay packet home?' When she finally found out my grandmother was contemptuous of what she saw as yet another frivolous decision and said that she was leery of hospitals.

'At least she'll find it a lot more enjoyable,' ventured my cousin Margaret calmly, 'Because she'll still be helping people but she'll get paid for it.'

In fact there was very little pay and nothing pleasant about Gravesend & North Kent Hospital. It was a purpose-built Victorian building with a darkly ominous frontage. The green and brown tiling in its long narrow corridors seemed permanently grimy and even flat rubber soled shoes seemed to clatter and echo on the ancient linoleum. Quite apart from all that it was where my father had suddenly died five years previously. I had immediate doubts about the place from the moment I was issued with the summer uniform; two pale blue cotton dresses with nipped in waists and buttons that strained across my breasts urging them to struggle for escape. I courageously complained to the woman who was in charge of 'distribution & supply' that I had been given the wrong size but was told nothing could be done until the winter uniforms were issued.

'You're just a bit stout,' my mother rightly observed and filled every fibre of my being with seething hatred.

'You're getting chunky,' my hated cousin Patsy hissed.

At least I had a friend at the hospital. Maureen Barlow from primary school who had expressed a keen desire for nursing from the age of five and positively glowed with delight when she wiped up vomit and emptied bed pans, was thrilled to welcome me. When I compared her enthusiasm with my own lack of it I realised there might be serious doubt about Reverend Mother's assurances and almost wished to be back among the Mercy Nuns. I most definitely did not want to be a nurse and wondered how difficult it was going to be to extricate myself from yet another bad situation. I need not have worried because within six weeks the hospital decided I was surplus to their requirements. It was all to do with fainting when practising injection techniques on a ripe orange; from Jaffa if my memory is correct. The Matron, a Reverend Mother Look-Alike, said extreme empathy for oranges was not an admirable trait and one to be discouraged in novice nurses. It came as a great relief and I was very pleased to hand back the ill-fitting uniform.

I returned somewhat sheepishly to Francis, Day & Hunter to ask if the job in the Copyright Department was still available. Surprisingly it was! Mr Blackburn looked a little sterner than he had at the previous interview and said that he hoped this time I had made up my mind about my future. I told him that I definitely had and he then said that a good shorthand typist could rise through the hierarchy and even become secretary to a person such as himself. I decided on the spot that there my future lay and pictured a more willowy me in the smart black skirt and crisp white blouse of Pat, his present secretary, busily transcribing Pitman's into page after page of faultlessly typed Copyright matters to be delivered to the four corners of the earth.

So it was I cheerfully joined the amorphous surge of Gravesend commuters who boarded the fast train to Charing Cross at 8.10 am on the following Monday morning. Reassuringly there were a few girls from school also intent upon employment somewhere more exciting than Gravesend and we huddled together in the corridor, all the seats already being taken by commuters from Rochester, Chatham and Gillingham, and tried to look sophisticated in our new skirts and Cuban-heeled shoes. Back then a large part of the group of working men heading towards London were City workers and wore the uniform that has long disappeared from even the most conservative of workplaces. Black bowler hats, overcoats and rolled umbrellas, all carrying a copy of The Times, almost impossible to read within the confines of a crowded commuter train. Their hands nudged their neighbours' as they struggled to concentrate on anything other than the front page, which then featured no news stories and was merely columns of advertisements. In the crush these males did not speak a single word, each ignoring his identically dressed and occupied neighbours. In contrast we girls chattered and giggled together just as we had in the fifth form. I told them highly exaggerated versions of my flirtations with the nunnery and with nursing, featuring incidents that bore little relation to truth and they looked at me in grudging admiration. Thereafter most of our conversation was directed at slandering other girls who were either still at school, having shown a degree of academic aptitude, or destined for a humdrum working life in the offices of Gravesend.

  The 8.10 express flashed through the rustic stations of Northfleet, Swanscombe, Greenhithe and Stone Crossing, the first stop being Dartford where a new swell of passengers pushed their way into the corridors. Brief glimpses of another half-dozen stations as we hurtled towards the next stop, Woolwich, within London itself where we became even more hedged in on every side by yet another group of determined train travellers. Then within minutes we reached London Bridge where the carriages began to empty, then Waterloo where those who had connections to Surrey to make, disappeared, and finally Charing Cross and the heart of London proper where each workday morning I felt my ongoing voyage of discovery really began. The station concourse was then, and very possibly still is, a seething cauldron of purposeful commotion at that time each weekday morning. The bowler hats mostly turned right towards Fleet Street and The City. Dark grey suited travellers turned left towards Whitehall and clutches of young women with neatly permed hair and 'swagger' jackets in various hues jostled each other towards the illuminated sign and down the steps into the underground which at that time was called 'Strand' and could be entered from within the station itself. I eagerly merged into the queue for one of the dispensing machines, anxious to tip in the coins required and receive the pale green ticket that permitted me to travel the two stops to Tottenham Court Road.

It was at some point during those first few underground journeys that I entered into a complex love affair with the network, the flame of which has never quite extinguished. Navigating London can be daunting for the novice. The city is overwhelming, seeming full of people who know exactly where they are going and how to get there, the newly-arrived hovering helplessly on street corners with bewildered expressions on their faces, clutching maps and advice flyers from London Transport. The red buses, although immediately recognisable and iconic, are themselves unfriendly and unforgiving and to board one is to risk ending up in places that can often seem hard to retreat from. The Underground on the other hand is easily navigable with a schematic map and clear colours denoting the various routes, which in the nineteen fifties were rather fewer than they are now. My line, the Northern Line, was solidly black and you could if you so wished travel all the way from Morden in the South to Edgware or High Barnett in the North without getting lost and end the day with the satisfaction of having crossed the mighty metropolis without incident. And within a week or two I did just that, illicitly on a two-penny ticket taking care not to exit at any of the possible and tantalising destinations. More daringly on a more legitimate ticket you could even get out along the way, perhaps at Clapham South or Chalk Farm and have a look around, taking care not to wander too far from the reassuring red circle at the station entrance. And I took those journeys too in time. However, on my first working day, I simply headed towards Tottenham Court Road anxious to arrive a little before the starting time of nine thirty.

The underground has its own atmosphere, a quality peculiar to itself and upon descending the very first escalator you can, if you are sensitive to atmosphere, start to smell it and can almost reach out and touch it. There was then a sensation of sootiness on each platform and a faint greasy slick adhering to the tiles that somehow inexplicably remains today, its essence forever trapped within the core of newly constructed and astonishingly unpolluted destinations such as Westminster and Canary Wharf. It was and is a specific ambiance that transcends reason and gives the subterranean city an analogous and parallel persona, similar to the city above but at the same time sufficiently different to keep its regular inhabitants at all times wary as they might be in a disquieting dream about a familiar place. It was always evening in the underground because it sported only an artificial light, never quite bright enough to make reading easy. This was not a problem to most peak hour travellers as the carriages on the Northern Line were then packed to capacity making any idea of reading totally impossible.

I arrived early as I had hoped at 138 Charing Cross Road and although all the ground floor shop staff were present and poised ready to sell sheet music and 78 rpm discs, there did not appear to be a single customer on the premises. I had during the intervening months of convent and hospital forgotten the way to the back stairs entered via the alleyway to the right of the building and therefore made my entrance through the grand glass doors fronting Charing Cross Road.

'I'm the new typist for the Copyright Department.' I addressed the most senior looking of the shop staff. He ushered me towards the grand staircase to the rear. From the first floor the young woman in the switchboard kiosk who also acted as general receptionist directed me to more stairs and so I progressed rapidly almost to the top of the building.

Mr Blackburn's secretary Pat, of the crisp blouses and slim skirts, introduced me to Mr Farr, Mr Chipperfield, Mr Davis and Mr Benson who were already before their desks in various corners of the room, studying matters of copyright. It seemed that although I would be typing some letters for Mr Blackburn himself if Pat became overwhelmed by his daily demands of her, for the most part my job would be to type for these four gentlemen. However before any of that could happen I had to be taken on an introduction tour around the building and we started from the floor above where the musical Arrangers and Copyists, David and Eric worked under the direction of Mr Young. This was also where Flo the tea lady spent most of her time preparing morning coffees and afternoon teas and showing snaps of her little grand-daughter Julie. Pat told me that Flo had `been on the halls' as a younger woman and now though forced to take a more mundane job liked to keep as close to the world of musical variety as possible. For instance she would never consider working for a Shipping Company or a group of Chartered Accountants.

In the packing department a number of men in blue overalls worked and the only one I remember was the one called Bill with a lame leg who later in that week exposed himself to me and asked me what I thought. Because I had not been so brazenly confronted with this part of the adult male anatomy before, all the molesting cousins being more modest, I giggled and flounced away, not sure of the correct or acceptable reaction, anxious only to be seen as mature and sophisticated. This incident took place in a manner that in these more enlightened and progressive times would give rise to horror and talk of court appearances. However, in the nineteen fifties such matters were simply blips in the working day for teenagers like me with large breasts and low self-esteem.

Opposite the packing department was a small, cramped office that Pat told me was not strictly part of Francis, Day & Hunter but a separate publishing company renting space in the same building, Mellin Music. She said she would introduce me to Tony who was nearly as new as me and about the same age. Tony was a rather good-looking young man with dark Spaniel eyes and a mop of unruly curly hair. He was Mellin Music's new office boy and readily agreed he had been a schoolboy until a week or two previously. He seemed very shy and shuffled his feet self-consciously so I smiled kindly at him in what I hoped was a big sisterly way. When I met him again some years later he had already almost turned into the celebrated performer and musician Tony Hatch and did not seem shy at all. In the Professional Department on the first floor someone called Johnny was thumping out a popular song on the piano whilst a mean-looking middle-aged woman with a poodle sang along enthusiastically. I met Stella and Olive who worked for Mr Jones and Mr Corrie who were the men who met pop stars on a daily basis and were invited to film premieres and very occasionally flew to Paris or New York. I was not introduced to the men themselves because they were far too busy and important. But I was formally introduced to Joan of the switchboard who in turn took me into the office of the elderly Miss Want, secretary to Mr David Day himself, a remote figure who did not appear each morning until after ten and lunched on a regular basis with the rich and famous.

Francis, Day & Hunter Ltd, founded in 1877, was something of a giant in the music publishing field. Two of the originators, James and William Francis, had both previously worked with Chappells in Bond Street, itself founded as long ago as 1810 and considered the elderly statesman of the business. Eventually they left Chappells to try their hand as performers and to this end they became friendly with a certain Harry Hunter who operated a Music Hall and was also a dab hand at song writing. Along the way they met the Day brothers and the group took premises in Oxford Street to open their own shop front and song publishing business as Francis, Day & Hunter. The industry had grown naturally out of the light music and classical fields and as time went on became a separate entity, eventually finding itself in the general environs of Denmark Street to be regenerated as Tin Pan Alley.

In the mid nineteen fifties a great deal of sheet music was still sold, not only to performers but also to members of the public and pianos still graced many a front room or parlour even in Northfleet and Gravesend. As early as 1910 John McCormack was signing his first contract with Victor and singing his heart out to the delight of my grandmother and her cronies who then occasionally sang outside pubs themselves when short of a bob or two. LPs and EPs were developed in the late 1940s and by 1952 retailers like Francis, Day & Hunter, had neat rows of them alongside the cheaper and of course more accessible 78s which we called `singles'. I arrived in Tin Pan Alley at a time when Bill Haley had already had a raging success with *Rock Around The Clock* and Elvis Presley had recently released *Heartbreak Hotel.* I was not a collector of records, 78s or otherwise as I did not own a record player of any description although I had a number of relatives who did.

'Once you've been here three months you can buy 78s and 45s from the shop at a special price.' Pat was saying as we ascended the stairs back to our own domain. At once I determined to make an investigation of becoming the owner of a record player a priority.

'You take a turn one day a week on the switchboard at lunchtime to relieve Joan,' she added as an afterthought.

'The switchboard?' I was immediately nervous. I had never used a telephone in my life. The only people I knew with telephones were the priest, the doctor and the proprietor of the corner shop.

'What will I have to do?' I tried to sound off-hand reflecting that the most recent of the mythical families I invented on a regular basis to replace my real family, would undoubtedly be all too familiar with the telephone. There was no good reason why they should not be. Even I knew it was a social convenience that had been around for decades so they might even have an upstairs extension as well as the phone in the hall, perhaps in my mother's bedroom. I had very recently decided that her name was Kate and her bedroom was pink and gold with huge built-in wardrobes to hold her clothes.

Pat's heels were clicking efficiently over the parquet, 'You answer calls and put the callers through to those they want to speak to. You'll find it perfectly straightforward because it's really just like answering the phone at home.'

She could not know that there was a hurdle or two for me to leap and that there were families that aspired to a television set before a telephone. However the hurdle leaping was not going to happen until Thursday and today was Monday so the problem could be safely shelved in the interim.

When we were settled behind our desks once more, Pat told me that when I was unable to start immediately after my interview earlier in the year Mr Blackburn had got a Jamaican girl on trial from an employment agency and she would still have the job had she proved to be reliable. Melinda was her name and although she had been punctual for the first week after that she had reliably turned up ten minutes late every day and Francis, Day & Hunter could not accept that level of capricious disregard of the rules no matter how willing they were to welcome a woman of colour onto their staff.

Melinda! What a delightful name. It was at that moment I decided to have a change of name myself and told her that it had been intended to christen me Antoinette and therefore I had always been known as Toni. Toni I felt was a name with all the elements necessary for a trendsetter, even a sophisticate. Toni did not sound like a gormless schoolgirl. Pat accepted the name change without query and said she would be sure to let everyone know.

She then said it was lunchtime and led me half the length of Oxford Street to sample the delights of a Forte's hamburger where we stood crammed together alongside a high chrome bar where luckier patrons perched on chrome and black stools. She asked me about my family and I abandoned Kate with her pink and gold bedroom and instead told her about a newer and cautiously modest family with a semi-detached interwar house inherited by my mother from an aunt. The house needed modernising but since her marriage break-up my mother, whom I decided to call Sue, had not really been in a position to attend to this. She would like a better kitchen and a fitted cocktail cabinet in the lounge. Still, there were some attractive features that we would keep, like the stained glass windows in the hallway that lit the stairs when you ran up and down them. A lot of people thought Art Moderne features were ugly, I said, but I really liked them. Pat was not listening very attentively. She had finished her coffee and was patting her lips on a paper napkin. I pictured myself sitting on the stairs of the interwar house, totally alone early in the morning shoulders drenched in a multitiude of colours as the sun rose. At times, I thought, the house reminded me of a church.

That afternoon Mr Blackburn asked me to take some dictation and my nervousness was soon dispelled because of the slowness of his delivery. I typed the three letters, all concerning pieces of music to be played in the theatres of Sydney and Melbourne, in no time at all and by that time it was four o'clock and Flo was distributing cups of afternoon tea and ginger biscuits. This business of working for a living, was distinctly easier than life in the Fifth Form where each evening homework assignments had loomed over me, completely disturbing my equilibrium. It was also infinitely preferable to the demands of Convent life where the obligation of extended periods of prayer and contemplation were time consuming. And it was a serious step up from nursing. Nevertheless it did bring with it new concerns and worries such as the fear of Thursday when I would be obliged to spend one hour on the switchboard on the first floor as Joan's official Lunch Relief. Wednesday evening I did not sleep at all and almost decided not to go to work at all the next day when I hit upon the splendid plan of delaying the nasty business for a week by pretending to have lost my voice and addressing everyone in a hoarse whisper all morning. Pat obligingly took over my duty that first week which was an enormous relief but only a temporary one because of course I had to face the dilemma the following Thursday. I felt a bit like one of the early Christians about to face a pride of lions in the arena when I presented myself pale and trembling to Joan ten minutes before midday so she could give me a quick lesson on the mysteries of the switchboard. Within a minute or two she placed her headphones deliberately before her on the bench among the tangled accumulation of cords and cables that I was imminently supposed to make some sense of. She looked at me and said, 'You're phone shy aren't you? That's what the problem is.'

Phone Shy! It sounded shameful and I was not at all certain what it meant. I nodded. She asked, 'Have you got a phone at home?' and feeling more humiliated by the minute I admitted the terrible truth. She began what turned into a thirty minute tutorial whilst, not for the first time, I racked my brain to think of anyone in our large working class and almost proud of it family who would at any stage consider a telephone could be of any use to them. Except me of course. Being outed as one who was phone shy did not prevent me from the ongoing fantasies of vaulting into a more conveniently conventional and attractive family group.

Apart from the brief dalliance with Kate and her pink and gold bedroom, since leaving school I had generally placed them just below the strata of the middle-middle class. The rambling thatched cottages in Kent villages had been supplanted by nineteen thirties semi-detached Art Deco style residences on purpose built estates such as the one described to Pat. The houses were now close to the town centre in roads called Laburnam Close or Willow Walk. Gone were the stepfathers who drove sports cars and the mothers who were actresses and were now replaced with more honest, straightforward widows or divorcees who definitely worked for a living but certainly not cleaning other people's homes like poor Nellie. For instance I had given Sue a respectable job as a Senior Ward Sister in the local hospital wearing a blue cotton dress with a nipped in waist. Well paid and honest employment that would eventually allow her to make the improvements she so desired to the house with the stained glass in the hallway.

When Joan felt I had mastered the basic elements of controlling the switchboard she went off to a Lyons Tea Shop and left me to what was to become a quite thrilling weekly duty. Armed with a list of telephone numbers of the famous and infamous I obediently located those whom the important people in the Professional Department wished to speak to.

`....Get Miss Winifred Atwell on the phone for me dear....'

`....Find Mr Billy Cotton for me...'

`....Ring The Ivy and book a table for two for Mr David Day and Miss Christina Foyle...`

I the phone shy one found I could complete these undertakings without skirmish and at the same time had the exhilaration of actually speaking to the illustrious.

`....Is that Miss Winifred Atwell? Would you hold a moment I have Mr Tommy Sanders on the line for you.`

Working for a living was totally exhilarating! And there was still the whole of London to be discovered and explored in detail.

Within a few days I managed to avoid joining Pat for lunchtime hamburgers and instead set out in various directions from my central point at 138 Charing Cross Road, investigating the city around me and buying a bar of chocolate along the way to help with the hunger pangs.

My first venture was into the upper reaches of Tottenham Court Road where the vast emporiums of the furniture trade were just beginning to be joined by those selling radios and television sets, past the Dominion Theatre on the right which had replaced the old Court Cinema, closed as far back as 1918 on account of the Trading With The Enemy Amendment Act; apparently it had a German manager. I walked briskly along the theatre side of the road for exactly twenty-five minutes, at times deviating off to the right to investigate an alley or side street, up as far as the great and grimy Euston Road. Then crossed and retraced my steps on the other side which I later deemed to be the more interesting. More appealing primarily because of the tube stations, Warren Street and Goodge Street both on `my` line the Northern and whose names I had already committed to memory. These were the next two thrilling places along the route from Charing Cross, were the Northern Line traveller to decide not to get out at their usual destination after all. And because it all seemed so remarkable and stimulating I descended into each one and had a look around the ticket halls delighting in the knowledge that I could if I decided to do so, simply buy a ticket and return to Tottenham Court Road via the underground like any other laid back Londoner.

Next day I set off along traffic congested New Oxford Street and High Holborn, now an even busier thoroughfare between the West End and the City. Reaching Chancery Lane I passionately desired to explore it instead of going back to the Copyright Department of Francis, Day & Hunter but instead descended into the ever beckoning hall of the underground station marvelling at the fact that it was a Central Line station and could be reached via the Tottenham Court Road junction at any time I wished for the price of threepence.

Later in the week I could not wait to start heading along Oxford Street in the direction of Oxford Circus and Bond Street where the shop fronts along the way were so enticing I only reached the station entrance at Argyll Street before perilously crossing over to return on the North side. I regretted not reaching the world famous

Selfridges Department Store tantalisingly ahead, which was said by my worldly cousin Connie to have a reputation as a shoppers' paradise. She also spoke loftily of Bourne and Hollingsworth and John Lewis's as both having similar status. I was cautiously impressed with her shopping knowledge because she had once applied for a job in the perfume department of one of these emporiums before settling for a similar post in a very much smaller Gravesend version. On this first expedition of the original road to Oxford I firmly resisted the urge to duck into the beckoning narrow side streets, most especially so on the South Side because I realised, with a throb of eager delight that they would lead me into Soho.

I was saving Soho, the savouring of which I knew would take several lunch hour periods. I could see where Soho began from the windows of the Copyright Department. The narrow streets and alleyways arose abruptly from behind the building that was Foyles' vast bookshop and underneath the tired illuminated sign that informed the world that Damaroids was the Great Rejuvenator, leading me to wonder what Damaroids were or are and I still don`t know and they still sound vaguely indecent. The area was still fields when the first Queen Elizabeth was on the throne and named, I had read, after an old hunting cry - `So-ho…..so-ho….tally-ho` perhaps. Definitely handy for hunting as far as the Court at Whitehall was concerned and convenient for the old City itself. But an explosion of building took place after the Great Fire of London in 1666 and the area rapidly became home to hordes of the homeless. Over time it attracted disparate groups and since the war large numbers of Chinese were beginning to trickle into the area to join the even larger numbers of Italians, Poles, Jews and Germans who were already well established there.

The atmosphere of hustle and bustle on the narrow streets differed from the activity and commotion of the adjacent major thoroughfares of Charing Cross Road, Oxford Street, Regent Street and Shaftesbury Avenue enclosing the area. In Soho there was an immediate sense that a workforce breathed life into the place and that the workers actually lived nearby, simply stepping downstairs or along the street to go to work in market, workshop or café.

The delicatessens, patisseries and wine merchants were hard to pass by. Gravesend had at that time no delis at all and only one coffee bar. Here the smells of garlicky sausages swinging seductively in doorways mingled with the odour of soiled sawdust strewn over uneven floors and after a moment were gone to be replaced with a brief whiff of alcohol-saturated apricots recently turned into vast oval tarts, or pears standing in tall jars steeped in rum. In the early summer of nineteen fifty six walking those confined little streets with their reputation for sin was like floating in a bubble of unbelievable enchantment. The clatter and chatter was enormous and all-embracing for there were people everywhere, three or four it seemed in every doorway and little queues formed inside each shop as discerning customers chose exactly which olives or how much cheese to buy that day. Every second doorway harboured what were then known as 'business girls', which for a long time I thought meant shorthand typists like me. They were exotic-looking creatures in impossibly high heels and close-fitting low-necked sheath dresses in bright colours, smoking Sobranie Black Russian cigarettes. Until I somehow or other learned the true nature of the business they were engaged in I wondered how they could type effectively with their elongated and claw-like blood-red nails.

It took no time at all to stumble across the famous Two I's Coffee Bar in Old Compton Street, squeezed uncomfortably between a Deli and a Betting Shop. This was where you went to be discovered and propelled to Rock and Roll stardom or, more mundanely, simply to observe those about to be so. I was among the latter group of course as I expectantly entered the cramped basement and purchased my cappuccino and Rum Baba along with a dozen or more of the similarly curious.

An even more attractive lunch hour activity was to enter the buildings playing host to Rehearsal Rooms where pianos thumped out thin tunes hour after hour and the thud of dancers' feet were heard above them. And feeling daring I actually did so from time to time, climbing narrow, rickety staircases to gaze through half glassed doors that ordered the outsider Not to Enter or stated that a Rehearsal was In Progress. Of course no-one challenged me but I was in any case armed with my cover story; I was looking for Kerry Hamilton. I had no idea who Kerry Hamilton was but she sounded to me like someone who may very well rehearse a dance routine in an upper room in Soho perhaps even in preparation for an engagement at the Shaftesbury Theatre down the road.

Dancers and musicians gravitated to Soho and during the early afternoons showgirls oddly pale without makeup, hair scraped back from ghostly faces, emerged from Piccadilly Circus and Leicester Square stations, all wearing flat black 'ballerina' shoes and carrying little cream make-up cases with shiny black handles. Now and then I followed them, curious as to their destination and often they headed for the Rehearsal Rooms and sometimes to the very theatres themselves that stood on Soho's boundaries, swiftly entering Stage Doors and greeting people just within called Alf or Jim. I lingered without and envied them, wondering if I could transform Toni the shorthand typist into Antoinette the dancer. Although it was tempting to conjure up star quality, she did not have to become famous. She could simply be a chorus girl, leaving home in West London every day to attend early afternoon rehearsals for a West End show to open next month. Sadly, Sue and the Art Deco semi-detached would have to be dumped because Antoinette the dancer could not under any circumstances live in Gravesend. How on earth would she get home from the theatre each evening? The first props I would need though were some flat 'ballerina'shoes and a cream make-up case with a shiny black handle. I added them to my 'to buy' list.

Musicians loitered around the national headquarters of the Musicians' Union in Archer Street just around the corner from the Windmill Theatre. Sometimes they formed queues as if they were actually lining up for jobs which perhaps they were. More often they stood in groups on the pavement, exchanging information and promising to give each other a bell just as soon as the next gig was in the offing. It seemed in the nineteen fifties that Soho, whilst being at the core of the emerging coffee bar phenomena, was also at the heart of modern musical development via a conglomeration of basement clubs such as The Jamboree, The Flamingo, The Mandrake and The Bag O Nails. These places, almost as holy to me as churches, I investigated from a short and reverent distance and wondered if I would ever be fortunate enough to enter.

Lunch hour meanderings offered a quick familiarity with the West End and made me yearn to become a prominent part of it all. I was not altogether sure how this could be achieved whilst earning five pounds a week as a typist but drifted between feeling reasonably confident that something would be sure to turn up and descending into despair when nothing concrete appeared on the horizon. I remained balanced on the threshold of meeting the rich and famous, evidenced by those I was asked to locate by telephone on my Thursday Switchboard Relief sessions and after a week or two I looked back in some amazement at the fact that I had ever been phone shy at all. You definitely could not become a passing acquaintance of the noteworthy or those about to be so if you were hampered by phone shyness. And when I reached this undeniable conclusion whilst gloomily commuting back to Gravesend on the 7.20, I once again cursed the limits that my extreme working class background placed upon me. If it was not for Old Nan, Nellie, all the aunts and my many cousins all holding back my progress I could be at Drama School, even shortly to be offered juvenile leads in West End productions. At the very least I might be one of those sophisticated teens in dark duffle coats and black stockings observed in the coffee bars of Bloomsbury talking about preparing for auditions. There was no chance at all that any one of that group had ever been phone shy.

'We should get a telephone,' I said later that evening to my mother. We were sitting in the kitchen of the terraced cottage, with no laid on hot water and an outside lavatory that had been our home since I was born.

'What?' She looked amazed. 'What would the likes of us want a telephone for?'

'So people could ring us.'

'Why would anybody go out to the phone box in the cold just to ring us? Anything worth saying to us they can say when they run into us next at the shops or the bus stop.'.

'Well we could ring them then,' I said belligerently.

'You're just being pig headed. We don't know nobody we could ring,' she sounded confused. 'Except the doctor – and even then if you want him bad enough you can send somebody with a note for him to call.'

I said nothing and after a silence that was far too long she added, 'You'll drive me to Coney Hatch with your ideas you will.'

It was to be fifteen years before Nellie did have a telephone installed and it wasn't to be into the York Road terrace but instead into the Painters Ash Estate Pensioners' Flats where everyone else had one and talked at length about how their grandchildren rang them regularly on Sundays. Painters Ash also saw the dawn of the refrigerator, to my mother an extraordinary luxury. Until the middle of the nineteen sixties few of our neighbours felt the need for appliances such as refrigerators, washing machines, dryers, or even vacuum cleaners. The dawn of a television set in every home changed all that.

She took to the telephone much quicker than the fridge which for the first five years she preferred to switch off to save power and only kept the bread in it. The milk and butter still stood in a bucket of cold water inside the back door during the hottest months of the year. This was all in the future. In the moment that followed our discussion about the telephone I realised that there were times when I disliked my mother with a vehemence that was unnerving.

Special Hand Deliveries

My cousins Margaret, June and Patsy, were all older than me and Margaret was even married though rather unhappily it turned out. June was about to get married and Patsy was being urged to get married, having recently become pregnant. They all lived in Crayford, on a council estate built between the wars, conveniently close enough together to pop in and out of each other's homes at will. This council housing was grudgingly admired by my mother and she said it would certainly be a treat to simply turn on a tap for the ritual Saturday night bath instead of laboriously heating pans of water on gas stove and kitchen range. It would be almost true to say that at times the houses were very nearly admired by me too. They were a decided step up from unlovely York Road, hastily erected on the cusp of the 1848 Health Act, to house chalk quarry workers. Even so, it had to be admitted that even the York Road houses were an improvement on what had gone before them. The Act began to put an end to the 'Back-to-Back' housing that proliferated all over England to accommodate immigrant workers. Once country people heard they could earn twice as much in industry as on the land they simply walked to where they hoped to find fortune. The consequent demand for low cost housing was met almost entirely by speculators who recognised that there was a profit to be made from pocket-sized dwellings and built as many as was humanly possible on minute parcels of land. Prior to the Act houses had been built for as little as forty pounds apiece with the ubiquitous Back-to-Backs becoming even smaller than their tiny Georgian equivalents. It was generally agreed at the time that the relatively newly described 'working classes' were going up in the world when privileged enough to find themselves renting a post Health Act house such as those in York Road. The legislation ensured that there was access to the rear of the terraces so that ash and rubbish could be removed with some ease. It was becoming standard for each dwelling to have its own privy allocated to it and the yards at the rear had become marginally larger to make this possible. Some houses now even had the luxury of their own piped water, cold though it always was. And importantly, it was henceforth forbidden to keep livestock in backyards although it took time before the bye-laws followed that made this particular regulation enforceable.

I can only remember one of our immediate neighbours keeping a pig though most kept hens and even ducks were not totally unknown. It had to be said that the keeping of pigs was unheard of in Iron Mill Lane, Crayford and Aunts Maggie and Martha shuddered theatrically whenever the subject was touched upon, screwing their noses and foreheads in a manner intended to indicate that they barely remembered what a pig was. Even my grandmother managed to look briefly puzzled though we all knew that in her time she had found herself homeless on more than one occasion and sleeping with her young children beside a pig sty for warmth. They had been sleeping alongside the pigs at a farm in Mereworth the year she sold my mother's birth caul to a sailor in Whitstable for the enormous sum of three pounds. Nellie had been born in the hop gardens on the nineteenth of August nineteen hundred and eight, astonishingly `in the caul' or with the amniotic sac intact and covering her face and upper body. Such infants were said to be charmed and would never die from drowning and the cauls themselves were much sought after by sailors as good luck talismans because the holder of a caul would also avoid death by drowning. Old Nan was said to have had twenty-one pregnancies and although between us my cousins and I could never account for that many aunts or uncles, she did end up with at least thirteen live children, twelve of whom were girls. She was not a woman given to undue sentiment and throughout her life extended no loving gestures towards her children or grandchildren. If she had been wont to make one of her offspring the object of her affection or pride, however, it would have undoubtedly been Nellie. She was never averse to relating the story of my mother's unusual birth, the astonishing remarkable and intact caul and how a group of sailors had almost come to blows over possession of it. And when she did so an unusual note of tenderness might creep into her voice as she recalled the details.

`….and come end of September, we straight-way once the hopping was done and dusted, goes back and rents us a fine place in Maxim Road, Crayford, just round the corner from where we was chucked out… with more'n a month's rent down, in advance like....' she might say recalling the surprise of the landlord with some satisfaction.

There had certainly been times when the family was forced to become more than comfortably familiar with accommodation that involved living under tarpaulins on field edges in summer and against pens housing various animals, in winter. But now securely in their interwar council houses, large gaps had appeared in their collective memory. The estate houses were semi-detached with bay windows and entrances both at the fronts and sides. There were small hallways with hooks for outdoor coats, and upstairs each had its own bathroom with boxed in bath and matching easy-to-clean panels. There were mysterious and slightly alarming Ascot geysers with pilot lights above the baths and hand-basins conveniently placed close by, sharing the same plumbing. The walls of these wonderful spaces, that echoed when you went in and closed the door behind you, were half tiled in cream with dark brown borders. Most blissful of all were the modern whiter than white toilets positioned below matching enamelled high-level cisterns. All things considered it would be awkward to conjure up a more lavish bathroom style for Ward Sister Sue, my recently created mythical mother.

'D'you want to have a bath love?' My Aunt Maggie had taken to offering a hot bath from time to time when we visited and I could not work out if it was because she realised how much I admired her bathing facilities or whether I was simply smelly. Either way I usually agreed, my mother then instructing me to save the water and ordering Bernard to hop in after me which he did unwillingly. Old Nan who did not believe in too much washing and only rarely used her own bath for that which it was intended, would sniff contemptuously and say I'd wash myself away if I wasn't careful.

We were to spend the first Christmas of my working life as visitors in one or other of the Crayford estate houses and predictably, apart from the possibility of a bath or two, I was not looking forward to it. I was no fonder of family Christmases than I was of family holidays. At these jolly get-togethers the thoughts of males young and old on the periphery of the celebrations invariably turned to sex. Some of their onslaughts were more half-hearted than others but overall the problem had not diminished with the years and I was constantly watchful. I had long concluded this was behaviour that must be endured if it could not be avoided. Furthermore there was a lurking suspicion that it might be my own fault and I would definitely be in Big Trouble if anybody found out.

The common denominator between the various branches of the family that year seemed that they were all the proud owners of new radiograms and June's even had an auto-change that would reliably stack up six LPs and play them one after another. You could have music at their place all afternoon if you so wished without moving from your armchair. They all had the latest LPs of Guy Mitchell, Frankie Lane, Jo Stafford and Alma Cogan interspersed with Vera Lynn and Gracie Fields to appease the over forties. I was envious and Nellie said I ought to treat myself to one then but Old Nan was disdainful and said she wouldn't give one of them things house room not if they was giving them away – which, of course, they were not.

On Christmas Eve those who could not be described as children or teenagers got drunk and talked about going to Midnight Mass but didn't get around to it. So none of us went in the end. On Christmas Day we ate roast turkey and plum pudding with corn-flour sauce as usual and the significant excitement was when Margaret unwrapped the gift from her husband which was, astonishingly, a tape recorder. We then had a great deal of fun learning how to use it and recording conversations between the unwary.

'My Violet's got herself a lovely little job in Dempster's shop of a Saturday.' This from our grandmother, sitting with folded arms so close to the fire it seemed her hair and clothing might become delightfully singed at any moment.

'A job? At her age? She ain't even twelve yet,' Nellie sounded disbelieving.

'Old Mother Dempster's a right Ikey Mo,' Martha flicked ash from the end of her cigarette, 'A tight fisted cow she is.'

'I see that oldest Dempster girl down the co-op last Saturday. A right slommuck she is too,' Maggie was pouring Cherry Heering into the little blue-green glasses won at a funfair in Margate before the war.

'I reckon the poor cow is carrying again,' this in a low voice from Nellie and pregnant Patsy at once sat up straight in her chair, completely alert.

'Never – she's only just dropped one…..a month back it was,' Maggie's turn to be disbelieving. 'She can't be up the duff again surely?'

'She brought that one in to see me back last Friday week' Nan now concentrating on fashioning a thin roll-up from the newly opened coil of Old Holborn removed from her apron pocket.

'Is it a boy or a girl?' Patsy was curious

'I dunno,' the roll-up was completed to her satisfaction so she placed it between her lips, 'Cor blimey it's bleeding ugly though – frightened the life out of me it did.'

Patsy said she couldn't see how a new born baby could be ugly enough to frighten anybody but was told by her mother, Martha, to keep her trap shut and not give any more old lip when her elders and betters were talking.

Freda, the youngest aunt and mother of two illegitimate children gave Patsy a brief look of satisfaction and said, ' She worked down Vickers that oldest Dempster girl did – Ivy, that was her name. I never took to her. Smarmy cow to my mind….'

'Well you'd know all about smarmy.' Patsy's final comment as she flounced from the room.

Margaret and I found these exchanges very amusing and Bernard was fascinated with the technology but Nan said we gave her the pip. A day or two later on the bus back to Northfleet Nellie announced she didn't hold with all that recording nonsense and when Bernard suggested I should invest in a tape recorder rather than a record player she scoffed and said that anybody with an ounce of savvy would much rather have a record player.

'I'm going to get one when the sales start in January,' I said, breathing onto the bus window and drawing a small Christmas tree.

'What, a tape recorder?,' asked Bernard.

'No – a record player, stupid!'

I was feeling buoyant having flown through the festive season assault free. It gave me cause to wonder if it would now stop altogether, even at work. After the incident with Bill with the lame foot some months before, I had taken care to avoid the packing department if at all possible. However there had been a copy-cat event a week or two later at the rear of the shop one morning where a handsome young man whose name was Cyril was busily counting sheet music.

'Well – what d'you think of this fella then?' he asked conversationally. Cyril was very tall and he laid the part of his anatomy I was supposed to admire on the sorting bench before him.

'Not much,' I said with a nervous giggle, and he put it away again and carried on counting.

I wondered, not for the first time, if the same thing ever happened to Joan of the switchboard or to Olive and Stella but decided that for some reason they all commanded more respect than I did in the working environment. Even in my very first week young Mr Farr, tall, dark and also reasonably handsome had observed, looking straight at me, 'You're alright from the neck up only.'

I gave my usual anxious laugh, 'Why is that?'

'Because you're too fat.'

I went puce with humiliation before saying in as offhand a manner as I could manage that it was just puppy fat.' He said that he would not want a puppy my size.

There is no easy way of being a fat teenager and I had been steadily gaining weight since my eleventh birthday, nibbling away at anything edible as a schoolgirl when I had no money to indulge myself with Mars bars or Kit Kats. Having reached the dizzy heights of a regular wage earner these luxuries now accompanied me each evening onto the home bound train. Every Sunday evening I vowed the coming week would herald the start of my diet but invariably by Monday afternoon I was opting again for fat-disguising clothes. Like many overweight teens I thought I did a very good job of concealing the layers of blubber beneath loose blouses and long obesity-obscuring scarves. For some reason I assumed that the casual onlooker would not realise where the garments ended and I began. The day Mr Farr made his first observation on my weight I decided to approach the problem more scientifically. Instead of buying a Mars Bar that evening I would make a short stopover at the weighing machine at Charing Cross that promised, 'Your weight for one penny'. Unfortunately I had not noticed that the machine in question was of the 'I Speak Your Weight' variety and to my mortification at six thirty all and sundry in the vicinity became acquainted with the fact that I weighed twelve stones and nine ounces. The following day I gave up bread in favour of healthy Swiss wheat crackers because the slender young woman on the side of the packet assured the buyer that she kept her shape by consuming vast quantities of them. They did not work for me. I was clearly destined to remain obese.

In January I made a big decision and decided against the record player. Instead I would buy a typewriter. I was intending to somehow or other find an outlet for writing if it was possible and in any case I wanted the comfortable familiarity of having the typewriter, technology I completely understood, nearby. In some ways it represented freedom and autonomy. I could safely hunch over the typewriter hour after hour and there was no danger of it commenting on my general appearance or sexually molesting me.

They were not cheap. I spent several Saturdays in typewriter shops studying prices and performance. I would buy a portable machine, possibly an Olivetti which I had already been allowed to try in the shop in the road above the station in Gravesend.

It was twenty six pounds. A huge sum to me at that time and my mother came with me to sign a hire purchase agreement because at sixteen I was five years too young to do so. The saleswoman was slight and trim wearing grey, with grey permed hair and grey rimmed glasses. She had a plumper, younger companion who sat at a desk and simply answered the telephone. There were no calls during the time we were there and I wondered if there ever were more than one or two a day and if the plump young woman had started off being phone shy like me and how many calls about typewriters it took to stop her being so afflicted.

'It's a lot of money,' said Nellie looking uncomprehendingly at the hire purchase agreement and anxiously at the Olivetti.

The trim grey woman flicked a non-existent fleck from her cardigan and pointed helpfully to the space where she should sign.

'Twenty-six pounds is a lot to take out of one's capital,' she agreed, nodding companionably as Nellie signed, slowly in her childish hand. I had only vague notions as to what the word capital really meant but if I had twenty-six pounds to my name and available for spending surely she must realise I would be paying cash for the machine and not buying it on the never-never.

'Now we will need you to come in each week and pay one pound off the debt,' she had turned to me and was looking at me rather earnestly and speaking very deliberately in tones usually reserved for those who are slow witted. I wondered why they would let someone as dense as they thought me to be owe them twenty-six pounds in the first place.

I heard myself say far too loudly, 'I think I'll pay you three pounds today if that's acceptable to you – I really hate having too much debt hanging over me.' That was, I decided, what a person with a significant amount of capital might say – if indeed the word meant what I thought it meant. Under those circumstances they surely would not bother to make the tiresome trip to the Bank on the New Road to withdraw cash.

She readily agreed and took my three pound notes, signed more paperwork and we left the shop thanking her, with the Olivetti in its smart carry case and lots of bits of paper relating to its purchase. I could hardly wait to get home to try it out. The previous day I had taken the precaution of stealing a quantity of pale pink and pale blue copy paper and several leaves of carbon paper from the stock in my desk at 138 Charing Cross Road. I had already investigated the price of a ream of typing paper and had been appalled at the cost. Nevertheless I rationalised that eventually a successful novelist would just have to absorb the cost and with luck it should not be too long before I was successful.

That evening I began my novel about time travel in which the teenage heroine, a drama student who had been awarded a scholarship to RADA, finds herself to-ing and fro-ing between Bloomsbury and Ancient Egypt where I could not decide whether she should be a slave girl or a princess. I had read in an instructive library book giving hints as to the structure of the novel, learning that each chapter must be planned in advance almost paragraph by paragraph to neatly fit the already well calculated plot. Unfortunately all this forward planning did not come easily to me and so poor Maria/Cloella lurched uneasily from the squares of Bloomsbury to the banks of the Nile as she encountered one obstacle after another. I now remember very little about this possible best seller except that it is unlikely it was ever completed.

On Monday I became easily immersed once again in the day to day machinations of the music publishing business known to those who were not newcomers like me simply as 'The Business' as if in fact it was the only trade or industry worthy of any kind of mention. 'Ever since I've been in The Business…..' and 'They've been in The Business for years' tripped so effortlessly from the tongues of the sophisticates who worked for the song pluggers in the Professional Department that it was as if other forms of commerce and industry simply did not exist or if indeed they did then they were somehow of a lower echelon. This unbridled arrogance was infectious and I found myself gazing contemptuously on the underground at those unfortunates who were forced to toil in hospitals or department stores or type for accountants and importers. How pitiful their working lives compared with my own. I who was privileged to co-ordinate via the telephone, tables for those notables who wished to eat lunch at The Ivy. Well, once a week on Thursdays at least because if I was to be totally honest there was little chance of conversing with anyone of note from my desk in the Copyright Department. Once I recovered from the thrill of writing letters concerning *The Man Who Broke The Bank At Monte Carlo* to theatre or radio station executives in Sydney, Auckland or Toronto, the work was almost mundane. Such compositions were far too old fashioned to be of any interest to me and I recalled with some embarrassment that this particular ditty was a favourite of Old Nan and to my eternal shame I was more or less word perfect in it myself presumably because I had heard it so often over the years.

The place where I really wanted to type was the Professional Department on the first floor where Stella and Olive reigned supreme in immaculate eye make-up and dresses from Bourne and Hollingsworth. Oh the joy of being able to type for a song plugger! Though until I walked through the glass doors at 138 Charing Cross

Road of course I had no knowledge whatsoever of what a song plugger was. I rapidly learned and became full of admiration for these lofty individuals and their impossibly glamorous typists. A song plugger spent his day persuading singers and band leaders to perform the particular songs recently published by the company he worked for. He worked his charm most diligently upon radio disc jockeys and was often seen lunching with them in the Italian restaurants of Soho. He wore suits in light colours and daring ties and sometimes draped expensive knitwear from his shoulders. Until the nineteen forties apparently the pluggers had not been averse to offering bribes known as plug money but at some stage that became unacceptable. These dazzling personages had generous expense accounts and met people for drinks which they always paid for, at odd times during the day. Radio was of supreme importance and so they regularly walked through the sacred entrance of Broadcasting House in Langham Place and were not challenged because they were on familiar terms with the reception staff.

When I made my own humble entrance behind the scenes into the glittering business of Tin Pan Alley the epitome of success for any song plugger was to have his latest number featured on *Desert Island Discs* and those who managed this were spoken of in hushed and deferential tones. The programme had first appeared in January 1942 when Vic Oliver discussed with Roy Plomley his choices of musical entertainment should he be condemned to spend the rest of his life on a desert island `with a gramophone and an endless supply of needles'. Each guest could make eight choices and generally the guests were such that popular music did not feature large in their lives. It would be also be safe to say that Roy Plomley was not the average run of the mill disc jockey and was given to having guests like A.E. Matthews and Field Marshall the Viscount Montgomery of Alamein. The closest he came to Tin Pan Alley was probably the day he interviewed Eddie Calvert, also known as 'the man with the golden trumpet'. Being featured on his programme, therefore, was success indeed. Only a decade or so previously, DJs were known by the BBC as 'presenters of gramophone record recitals' but after the war this formality changed very rapidly and by my time regular plugging opportunities existed with the advent of programmes such as *Family Favourites* and *Housewives' Choice, Record Round-Up* and *Record Rendezvous.*

The important BBC DJs of the time were Jack Jackson, Sam Costa, Jack Train, Jack Payne, Eamonn Andrews and David Jacobs, all of whom seemed to me to be not quite human. When these exceptional beings were glimpsed entering or exiting the Professional Department in the company of Mr Spence or Mr Corrie, my heart thumped in my chest. The real gods though were the staff of Radio Luxembourg; Geoffrey Everitt, Teddy Johnson, Pete Murray, Keith Fordyce and Barry Aldiss and they rarely visited the premises but assignations were made with them at places like The Mirabelle Restaurant on Curzon Street. How I longed to be in a position to exchange pleasantries with these giants of Pop Music.

Then, completely out of the blue, a miracle happened when Bob the office boy's jaw was broken in a weekend fight. As the next most junior employee I was called downstairs by Olive and charged with the actual hand delivery of a package, presumably containing discs, to Pete Murray to his home which from memory was at the time in Norfolk Crescent near Marble Arch.

'Mr Blackburn says we can borrow you for an hour to make a special hand delivery,' she said, handing it to me, 'You take the tube to Marble Arch and walk up Edgware Road then the crescent is on your left. I'd do it myself but I'm snowed under this afternoon....'

What sublime bliss that Olive should be so snowed under. I set off hardly able to believe my luck, descending into the underground station in ecstasy. What would these sad and ordinary people sitting opposite me on the Central Line train think if they knew I was not just one of them, but a special person charged with making a delivery of enormous importance to the famous and oh so wonderful, Pete Murray?

When I emerged from Marble Arch station the sun was shining brighter than I ever remembered it and the sky was impossibly blue, the leaves on the Plane trees exceptionally green. Whilst underground there had been a brief rain shower that now made Edgware Road look like a magical highway and ensured that the red of the London buses glowed with extra brilliance. Norfolk Crescent was exactly where Olive had said it would be. How wonderful it would be to live in such a crescent, being neighbour to the great and glorious Pete Murray.

The mission became idyllic when the great man himself opened the door to my third or fourth timid knock. So this extraordinarily important creature did not have minions to do these minor tasks for him. He stood there in a loosely belted off-white dressing gown, lower legs trickling bath water. His bare feet made damp outlines on the parquet. I pulled my shoulders back and held in my stomach with all my might. He must not notice I am only alright from the neck up. I spoke in my most up market voice, the one I had practised for years as a child; my posh voice, used in London but rarely now in Gravesend.

'Hello – I'm from Olive at Francis, Day & Hunter....'

A hank of gold-brown hair fell damply across his perfect forehead as he smiled a brief and indifferent smile, leaning casually against the door jamb and taking the package with his strong, tanned right hand on which pale blue veins were etched like those I had seen in paintings on the hands of Jesus. Behind him I caught a glimpse of white walls and stripped pine hall furniture. How divine to live within a white walled heavenly little house like this.

'Thank you sweetie...regards to Bert and Olive,' and then the door was closed again and his picture perfect personage disappeared once more perhaps to resume his bath. Or would such a special person as he actually take a bath? A shower might be more appropriate I thought and made my way back to the tube station hardly believing my good fortune to have met him, to have briefly even almost, but not quite, touched him. For a few short seconds Pete Murray and I had engaged in the day to day dealings of The Business together. He had smiled at me. From that moment, for many months the redoubtable Mr Murray was my favourite radio personality and the pre-war set at York Road was permanently tuned to Luxembourg when I was at home and I nonchalantly dropped his name into conversations not only with my incredulous family but also with my friends on the 8.10, exaggerating a little and making sure they knew that he and I though not exactly close, were apt to meet from time to time for 'business' reasons.

And the excitement was not completely over until Bob's jaw improved sufficiently for him to return to his cubby hole at the back of the shop, for I was given other similar delivery errands, to the Adelphi theatre with a large brown envelope labelled for the attention of Mr Al Read. Disappointingly there was no sign of the gentleman himself and I was forced to hand it over to a dour doorkeeper who took it with complete uninterest. I consoled myself with the fact that I had at least been able to step inside the stage door, standing in the very place where over the years dozens of variety stars had entered. Indeed the very place where the ghost of William Terriss, brutally murdered in 1897, was still said to appear. I had read somewhere that Terriss had been stabbed as he stepped through the stage door itself so all in all a most historic place. A few days later I was directed by Stella to return to the theatre with yet another large brown envelope, this time for Miss Shirley Bassey from Tiger Bay, in recent months emerging as a major singing sensation.

'Do you want me to actually give it to her? – or shall I just leave it with the man at the stage door?' I asked with as innocent a tone as I could muster.

'Well give it to her of course if you get the chance,' said Stella, 'But of course if she's not there you'll have to leave it at the stage door.'

I set off towards Maiden Lane, cheerfully complimenting myself on my Machiavellian cunning. It was a damp and grey late winter afternoon and the journey took me through what had become my favourite area of London, the historic by-ways of Covent Garden. The narrow streets were now, still in daylight, bereft but for hungry gulls and playing children but would verge on the beginning of noisier life as the Market itself began to vibrate into wakefulness. In those days people lived in Covent Garden, out of sight, in the cramped flats hollowed out of Georgian buildings and Victorian purpose-built tenements on the fringes of the area. I recall Newport Dwellings and Sandringham Buildings and at least two Peabody Estates. Peabody was a philanthropist of some note and later I discovered to my surprise that he was an American banker and had for some reason supplied funding to house the respectable poor in Wild Street near Drury Lane and Bedfordbury off St. Martin's Lane. These were most desirable residences as far as I was concerned though I was aware of the drawbacks of living there. The flats were small to say the least, with the kitchen serving also as the living room and often as the bedroom. The larger ones sported a tiny bedroom to the rear of the kitchen. There were several flats on each landing, all sharing one toilet and a washroom with a sink where you could do your weekly wash if you did not want to visit the bag-wash. For most they would have been infinitely less desirable than York Road but for me they had the spellbinding attraction of being in the very heart of the place that so fascinated me.

A few months previously I had been taken inside one of these cramped and smelly dwellings by Bob whose job I was now delighted to be doing. We visited his grandmother who had grown up there, one of a family of nine.

'Me mum and dad've now got a semi on an estate in Ilford,' he told me importantly, 'We've got our own bathroom and everything – an' a smashing big garden out the back. Me dad is growing all our vegetables as well as flowers for me mum'

'We've got a semi too,' I lied, 'Only not on an estate – it's private. We own it.'

He looked at me admiringly and said 'Blimey' and that he thought I must be a toff.

When we left the poky little flat he told me he was glad he didn't have to live in one of 'them old places' and I agreed whilst secretly envying the toothless old lady on the third floor.

Now, although the air grew frosty I sauntered slowly through St. Giles Churchyard, across Shaftesbury Avenue and into Monmouth Street, not taking the shortest route, anxious to make the journey last and to give Miss Bassey plenty of time to arrive at the theatre for her evening performance.

Market porters were beginning to pull carts and yell cheerful obscenities at each other in Shorts Gardens and

Endell Street. Occasionally a coarse comment I studiously ignored was directed at me. I lingered at Seven Dials simply because it was my most favoured spot in my favourite place and then took the route that would take me past the dimly-lit theatrical costumiers where I could make a study of the window displays. And as I progressed as slowly as possible, the market unfolded into a hub of energy, the shouts becoming louder and lights appeared here and there between the wagons and drays and the unmistakable smell of winter oranges masked that of yesterday's stale cabbage leaves. Finally I drifted down Bedford Street, past Henrietta Street and the offices of *The Lady* magazine, still brightly lit with shadowy people moving about the office rooms inside, to the corner of Maiden Lane itself. Turning left the rear of the theatre was on my right.

The man at the stage door looked up apathetically and jabbed a hand in my direction to take the envelope.

'I was told to give it to Miss Bassey personally,' I lied.

'Well she ain't in yet,' he said.

'I'll wait for her if that's alright.'

'Suit yerself luv.'

He went back to marking his pools and after a few minutes I went back into the street, determined to wait there, strolling in what I hoped was a casual way towards the Bedford Street corner again. It was then I saw her walking towards me in a dark blue belted coat with a fur collar and high heeled shoes. It was undoubtedly Shirley Bassey.

She was charming and indulgent when I enthusiastically delivered the package, telling me she always came by tube to Leicester Square station. She hoped I would be able to come to the show one night she said. She thanked me profusely for taking the trouble to deliver the piece of music by hand. And I went away marvelling that the great Shirley Bassey, now almost a household name, known by both Old Nan and Nellie and certainly all my cousins, actually travelled on the underground just like me!

When Bob returned to work with broken jaw still in evidence but with a cheerful manner, I was no longer required to make out of office deliveries so my only opportunity for star spotting was on my weekly switchboard stopover or on my way to the toilet on the ground floor. I made far more toilet visits than was necessary and was able to bump into minor celebrities like Bob Brown of the Stargazers and Anne Shelton currently singing her heart out with *Lay Down Your Arms*. Neither he nor she looked in my direction.

Each morning as I made my way up the stairs, excitingly Teresa Brewer's *Sweet Old Fashioned Girl* or Kay Starr's *Rock and Roll Waltz* blasted through the doors of Olive's office and I sighed with satisfaction that these sounds would never be allowed to sully the serene passages and halls of the shipping office where my school friend Shirley typed all day. In daily conversation on the fast train with Shirley and the other girls I made sure they became increasingly aware of the daily interactions that took place between celebrities and myself and if necessary invented just enough to keep them wide eyed and titillated.

'So you actually spoke to Doris Day?' Jackie Harrop looked both impressed and incredulous.

'Only on the telephone,' I said hastily, not wanting to admit that the long distance call placed on behalf of Mr Bert Corrie had actually been to an American publisher and was something to do with a composition once recorded by Miss Day and that fact I only knew because I had been so enthralled to call Los Angeles, that I curiously listened in on the conversation for a few moments.

'What did she sound like?' Mary Blake wanted to know. 'What did she say?'

I did not want to get into too many details of a conversation that had never taken place so I said, 'She just sounded like Doris Day that's all.'

I quickly moved on to Shirley Bassey and Jackie said she was tired of hearing about her and would rather hear more about people like Doris Day or even Frankie Lane because her favourite song of all time was still *A Woman In Love*.

As a group I was aware that my travelling companions were in danger of beginning to regard me more with suspicion and disbelief than admiration and envy.

Night Flight to Prague

Despite the illusion of glamour I had woven around myself and my lowly position as a junior shorthand typist, I was also increasingly mindful of a profound well of dissatisfaction that bubbled away inside and at times it was as if a limb had been, however painlessly, torn away leaving a throbbing vacuum where it had once been. Something intangible was missing and if it could be located then perhaps life would become wonderful. Occasionally I even longed to be back in the fifth form classroom comfortably contemplating an evening of homework monotony broken by hot cocoa at nine o`clock. The friends and acquaintances from school all had lives outside their workplaces. Most had boyfriends and some even planned engagement parties. They saved up to get married, and on Saturday evenings they went to dances at The Royal Clarendon hotel in Gravesend or The Bowaters Sports Club in Northfleet. Sometimes they asked me if I wanted to go with them but I always refused. Anyway the only dance I could do with any competence at that stage was the old fashioned waltz. It always seemed a better option to stay home and read a book or plan my own next best seller which at that time was shaping up to be remarkably similar to Francoise

Sagan's *'Bonjour Tristesse'* but rather more profound, my own goodbye to sadness. I felt Sagan and I had a great deal in common and yearned to be like her. Possibly it would be prudent to become an existentialist before embarking on my own novel of great suffering. I bought a black duffle coat from the Army & Navy Surplus Stores and tried to read Sartre.

Most Saturdays I took to making the best use of my weekly season ticket by taking a fast train to London on excursions of discovery. I usually told Nellie I was required to do extra work which not only involved typing and filing but also meeting stars of screen and radio along the way. She said they were getting their pound of flesh and I was a fool to let myself be put upon. I adopted a saintly expression and left as early in the day as possible.

With a whole glorious day in front of me I made in depth explorations of the areas that most attracted me and some that did not have quite as much appeal. On the first of these day trips I aimed to thoroughly investigate my much cherished Covent Garden and began with an early train so when I crossed The Strand and made my way towards the Piazza it felt as if the market traders had only just departed. The streets were still slightly damp from an early morning shower and they resonated in that strange way that suggests the clatter and chatter ceased merely moments before. I began from Covent Garden underground station itself, turning from there into Long Acre to give the Freemason's Hall a cursory inspection. From there, right into Bow Street and towards the Magistrate's Court which I had read somewhere was once the police station where the Artful Dodger was taken and where Oscar Wilde spent several weeks awaiting his Old Bailey trial.

It was a crisply chilly morning with a watery sun struggling to announce its arrival and very few people were on the streets. I hurried into Russell Street towards London's oldest theatre, The Theatre Royal Drury Lane. I leaned against one of the impressive pillars of the colonnade and fervently wished to be delivering a package to someone within. The front of the building looked forlorn and neglected and discarded fish and chip papers from the night before lifted gently beneath my feet. I tried to find the place where Charles and Mary Lamb gave literary parties and where Charles might have written his letter to Dorothy Wordsworth - `*...We are in the spot I like best in all this great city...Covent Garden is dearer to me than any Garden of Alcinous....*' I had no idea what a Garden of Alcinous might be but how passionately I wished these words had been written to me by someone like Lamb. How ardently I yearned to come across someone who loved this district as much as I did. What bliss to sit together and discuss this particular devotion. What more could anyone want? I shivered with the anticipated delight of happening upon such a person as I strolled into the Piazza, still in those days the heart of the fruit and vegetable market where Dickens had gazed longingly at pineapples he could not afford. This was where two of the great Coffee Houses frequented by Fielding, and Pope had once stood and were described as `emporiums of wit and seats of criticism'. Being unfamiliar with the writings of either, I gave myself a guarantee that I would rectify that sad state very shortly and went back into a reverie of why other people were so unlike me and why I couldn't conform and be more like them.

I successfully found twenty-seven Southampton Street where Garrick had lived and then slipped confidently into Maiden Lane which I was by now so familiar with, past the Adelphi Theatre and on to stand longingly for a moment or two in front of Rules Restaurant. It was as great and grand as ever and forbidding and impenetrable to humble office juniors on modest incomes. Years later when circumstances had changed a little it became my favourite restaurant. In 1957, however, the only thing about the place that I was familiar with was the fact that I had read that Dickens, Thackeray, Galsworthy and H.G. Wells all ate there on a reasonably regular basis. I supposed they did so once they had become noteworthy and could afford the not insignificant prices. Even shortly after nine on a Saturday morning Rules managed not to look in any way world-weary or jaded, displaying to the world a small but unrelenting glow of polished wood interior and the air of careless luxury that comes with catering over decades to those who can afford not to consult prices on menus. Then to nearby Chandos Place where Warren's Blacking Factory once stood and where young Dickens was paid one shilling a day to fasten bottles and label them. I wondered if he too had meandered these streets before and after his day's work contemplating a time when he might be able to afford to lunch at Rules. Did he also feel a turbulent emptiness inside and a pressing desire for life to offer something better? Did he wish to find other people like himself?

The Actors' church, St. Paul's, had already opened and after sitting in the gardens to absorb their atmosphere of being quite delightfully hidden away, I went inside whilst it was entirely deserted and slowly examined all the plaques, becoming in the solitude quite suddenly suffused with joy. It was this very saturation of ecstasy that urged me once in the direction of the Mercy Sisters and it was now with some horror I realised that little more than a year later, I only half believed in God. How fortunate for the good nuns that my Calling was doubted early in the process. In the ominous silence of the church I looked cautiously about me for the vengeful bolt of lightning that might strike for lack of faith but happily nothing happened and so I hurried outside before God changed His mind and into Rose Street to admire the exterior of the Lamb and Flag.

Back in Long Acre I looked for Stanfords, said to be map and travel book specialists, because it had been mentioned in *The Hound of The Baskervilles.* Years later I learned that they had also provided maps for Amy Johnson in preparation for her record-breaking flight to Australia. Later still when I was well and truly in love with the diaries of Samuel Pepys I spent half an afternoon on those same streets merely to meditate upon the fact that in 1668 he had excitedly bought a second hand coach somewhere nearby for the princely sum of fifty three pounds and had spent the whole afternoon and part of the evening watching it being painted bright yellow.

It was strangely easy to buy theatre tickets on a sudden whim from box offices shortly before performances were about to start and on my Saturday excursions I did so, always the cheapest tickets for matinee performances. In my diverse reading I had become aware that an aspiring actor or indeed performer of any kind should make it their business to see as much theatre as possible. The life of a performer was one I now seriously contemplated although I was not at all sure how to go about it, so regular visits to the theatre were definitely on my list of things I should do. During 1957 I saw a number of plays such as *The Seagull* and *The Mousetrap,* became acquainted with The Old Vic and even went twice to the Adelphi to see the variety show featuring Al Read and Shirley Bassey. I tried to convince myself that I had enjoyed all the plays but if truth be told *The Seagull* was not to my taste and I came reluctantly to the conclusion that I was not quite as clever or sophisticated as I would like to have been. This fact I knew would have to be concealed from those I wished to impress.

Meanwhile my fast train companions spent their Saturdays shopping for orlon cardigans which they wore reverse fashion, buttoned down the back. They dressed carefully for the Saturday night dances where, if they were not already romantically involved, they met a series of eligible young men. I was still paying for the Olivetti typewriter and so new cardigans were not a priority and in my wanderings of London streets I did not seem to come across young men, at least none who were interested in me. I was usually returning to Gravesend just as the school friends were getting on the Crete Hall Road bus in their flared skirts with their clutch bags under their arms, a throng of bright colours and excitement. Sometimes I was even on the same bus.

'What are you up to? – we're off to the dance.'

And I affected disinterest, 'Just going home – I've been to the theatre in London'- even if I hadn't.

'*Theatre?* ' they were faintly incredulous.

'Yes, Chekhov.'

'Who's he when he's at home? You coming to the dance?'

'God no!' but all the while I envied them and wished I was like them, content to be ordinary girls living ordinary lives and not gripped by the dangerous desire to be different. My mother would have liked that too. She was also most anxious for me to go to the dance.

'I'm sure I don't know what's wrong with you. You're just not like the other girls. Why won't you go to the dance with them? You'll never have no friends if you don't. Nobody decent will want the likes of you if you carry on like this....'

Then harking back to my last year of school and the episode concerning Barry the dumped boyfriend, 'I don't know why you had to go and break it off with Barry – he was a lovely boy. You might not get another chance you know....not the way you are.'

It was astonishing how early in life a girl could be deemed to be 'on the shelf' because although I was just rising seventeen years old she clearly saw me as headed for spinsterhood.

'Lots of the girls that was in your class are engaged now you know,' she was wont to point out morbidly.

And when the various aunts came for weekend visits there was always the loaded question, 'Is she courting yet?'

And no, she wasn't.

'What does she do up in London of a Saturday?' they were both astonished and curious.

'Goes to theatres and that,' Nellie responded in a low voice, self-conscious because who would want a daughter that did such things.

Old Nan wagged a warning finger in my direction whilst looking at my mother and saying mysteriously 'I always warned you Nellie that she's a right brahman…..that's what she is… and no good ain't going to come of her'

It was no time to expand on the topic of Chekhov.

'My Patsy was courting at her age – so was our June and our Margaret….' Aunt Martha said smugly.

And considering the pregnancy, firmly marching forward, I wanted to retort smartly, 'and look where all that courting got your Patsy' but didn't dare to.

'Even my Ann has got a little boyfriend,' said Aunt Maggie, then making the young couple sound like dolls' house dolls, 'lovely little fellow he is – name of Roger.'

'It's all that reading what does it,' Old Nan relentlessly pursued the topic, bringing up the R word and adding her particular mantra with pride, 'I never read a book in me entire life and it's done me no harm whatsoever.'

True, she was totally illiterate, signed her name with a cross and had in her advancing years become staunchly proud of the fact.

What joy to be a sought-after, firmly courted young woman. I swiftly conjured up a tall, fair young man called Guy wearing a sheepskin jacket and cavalry twill trousers, old enough to enter licensed premises with practised carelessness.

'Let's drop into the Punch Tavern for a pint,' he now suggested, parking the racing green 1956 MG, hood down, at an angle almost directly outside.

I knew what to order because last week I had asked Pat from the office what she drank when she went to pubs with her boyfriend. She said they didn't go to pubs much but when I pressed her admitted she drank gin and bitter lemon at her sister's wedding and quite liked it. Satisfied, I committed gin and bitter lemon to memory and wondered if I would like it also.

We fought our way to the bar.

'I'll have a gin and bitter lemon I said,' and hoped it was the right kind of drink for someone like me to order. It rolled off the tongue quite easily at least. I was wearing a short suede jacket and very high heeled shoes that I was able to walk in without a hitch. My legs looked fabulous.

The barman greeted us affably because Guy was well known in the place and in fact a couple of other young men called out greetings, which was not surprising as I had just made him quite a prominent crime reporter and given him a job on the Daily Telegraph.

'Bloody good story on Wednesday Guy,' said the legendary Duncan Webb, patting him on the shoulder and giving me a friendly nod. 'Toni must be proud of you.'

I smiled, happy in the golden glow of reflected glory.

We took our drinks to the fortuitously empty alcove seats in the corner of the pub closest to the door where we could be seen by all who entered.

'I wish you'd agree to come over to Prague with me darling,' Guy said, 'Can't tell you much about it but I'm following a lead in this international drug deals story... I'm taking a night flight.'

I considered the idea of a night flight to Prague whilst slipping off my jacket to reveal my stunning figure, shown to its best advantage in a cream cashmere sweater from a very expensive shop in Regent Street and was just about to reply when Old Nan poked me with her stick.

'I was just saying to yer Mum, It ain't natural of a Saturday night for you to be stuck in here with a book like a big ninny.'

And so I took the book up to the cold reality of the bedroom above to read in bed with the eiderdown firmly wrapped around me and resolutely re-summoned The Punch Tavern where Guy was now deep in conversation with Duncan Webb.

'You really are the only one we could trust with this part of the job,' Duncan was saying in a terse, low voice, looking from side to side as he spoke, 'You do realise it does not come without its dangers?'

Guy stared into his half-empty glass and said he had everything under control. Duncan patted his shoulder again and casually became re-absorbed into the main body of the pub where a number of other people were anxious to speak with him.

'What on earth was all that about?' I slipped the suede jacket back onto my shoulders and took the cork-tipped cigarette Guy offered me.

'It's safer for you not to know right now darling,' he replied and lapsed into a short tense silence before telling me that he should really go back to his flat to do some research. I nodded understandingly because I knew only too well that he was under a great deal of stress.

I tried to go back to my library book. The bedroom was very cold.

Guy had finished his beer, got back into the green MG, dropped me off at Charing Cross Station and disappeared to wherever it was he lived. I hadn't decided that yet but it would undoubtedly be somewhere central.

I was able to assess the idea of gin and bitter lemon as a suitable drink to order much sooner than expected when the entire Copyright Department along with Olive and Stella from the Professional Department was invited to be a guest audience at the Embassy Club in Bond Street where Miss Winifred Atwell was appearing in cabaret to play, amongst other things, a selection of Francis, Day & Hunter melodies. Pat explained that from time to time we were the lucky recipients of such invitations simply because we were privileged enough to work in The Business. There had to be an invited audience she said, because it was being filmed for television and the filming was to take place during the afternoon when the club was normally closed.

'We have to wear cocktail dress,' she said.

Fearfully I told her that I did not own a cocktail dress, whatever that might be, and she said a plain black dress would be quite alright with high heels and I should have my hair shampooed and set during the lunch break. She would take me to Michael's in St. Giles High Street because she was having hers done as well.

It was all very exciting but on the train home I began to worry about the plain black dress and where I could locate one. After much deliberation I reluctantly came to the conclusion that my mother's best black taffeta dress would have to do even though it had unhappy connotations having been bought for my father's funeral. Even worse, the dress in question had a belted waist and no fat defying features. Still, beggars could not be choosers.

'It will all be on television a few days later,' I told Nellie importantly. She looked doubtfully towards the ten inch screen acquired very recently from The Rainbow Stores on the never-never, that at long last graced the corner of the room.

'Even on our set?'

'Yes, on any set,' I was rather doubtful myself as to how it all worked because we were still coming to terms with being regular TV watchers, having been the very last people in York Road to own one. So in 1957 we were quite undiscriminating and we watched everything from *Andy Pandy* and *The Flower Pot Men* to *Sunday Night at The London Palladium* and *The Adventures of Robin Hood.* We were still in awe of the technology and when our screen went awry, as screens often did in those days, we called in Mr Layton from two doors up the street to adjust it for us. On those occasions Nellie invariably pressed a two shilling piece into his hand and loudly insisted that he get himself a pint because she was very grateful. If he accepted she then spent the following couple of hours cursing and castigating him for taking money from a poor widow who didn't have a man to do these little jobs for her. Still, she reliably told everyone she came across in the neighbourhood and of course all the aunts, that I was going to be appearing on television as part of an invited audience and that this was because 'it's something they do at her work up in London'. They all promised to watch.

The exciting day dawned and I packed the black taffeta dress and my Cuban heeled shoes in a carrier bag to save having to wear them on the train. Pat escorted me to Michael's the hairdresser and we both had a seven shillings and sixpence shampoo and set at lunchtime. This was a totally new experience for me and I was both fearful and fascinated as Michael himself transformed my uninspiring fast growing out Home Perm into something that looked more fitting for the Embassy Club. Young Mr Farr who was going to be our escort for the duration, cast an approving eye over us both and told us we looked very smart.

'You ought to have your hair done every week,' Stella said to me later as we waited outside the shop for the taxis that had been provided by the television company, 'It makes you look much older.' I was sharing a taxi with the three girls and the men were to follow in a second vehicle. During the ride up Oxford Street, I reflected that my previous and only taxi ride had been when I was about eight and some strange Greek Aunts came to visit, out of the blue, causing a great deal of strife between my parents, my mother at one stage describing them as doxies and trollops. But that was all a very long time ago and the taxi concerned had not in any way resembled the one I now found myself inside.

When we got to the club it was disappointingly empty and quiet. But the cocktail bar was open and fortunately could fulfil more mundane orders such as Halves of Light, Pineapple Juice and Gin and Bitter Lemon. Mr Farr and Mr Chipperfield who had split the cost of the drinks, shook their heads at one another and made disapproving noises and agreed that the prices were outrageous and by rights they should have been provided on the house. I was glad to be female and in those days not expected to concern myself with paying and so I could simply revel in the fact that I was at last inside licenced premises with an alcoholic drink in front of me. I sipped slowly and felt stylish wondering if I would ever learn to enjoy the taste. If only Guy could be here with me my happiness would be complete.

'This is my fiancé,' I might say to Mr Farr. 'We're off to Prague on Sunday...we'll be taking a night flight'.

I must try to find out more about Prague and flying in order to give the whole daydream more substance. I planned a Saturday morning visit to the library.

The bar at The Embassy Club was extensively mirrored and looked very chic in a plumply upholstered way. The camera crew took a long time setting up to their satisfaction and occasionally a young man in dungarees would put his head around the door and tell us, 'not much longer now.' Eventually we were ushered into the club itself where a group of musicians prepared instruments and looked at their watches. We sat at small round tables by the dance floor and waited to be told what to do next. Someone called Pierre who was dressed like a comic book waiter on a smutty postcard of the kind sent by aunts from Margate or Ramsgate said that when the music started we should get up and dance. I began to feel sweaty and anxious, handicapped as I was as merely a waltzer. Mr Chipperfield leaned towards me invitingly as the musicians launched into a light hearted Quickstep.

'I can only do a Waltz,' I hissed, feeling glued to the chair.

'Nonsense,' he said, pulling me to my feet, 'It's simple. Just follow me. Chasses, quarter turn, lockstep!'

And I valiantly did my best to follow him, acutely aware that I was not making a very good job of it. However, he continued to propel me around talking all the time about how simple it was and how well I was doing and effortlessly morphing into Guy, now minus the sheepskin jacket.

He was, of course, quite dazzling as a ballroom dancer and wore a dark lounge suit, white shirt and black bow tie. His shoes were highly polished, almost like patent leather.

'When this damned Prague business is over we must come here more often,' he was whispering in my ear and I nodded up at him.

I was wearing a full skirted silver evening dress that swished and swirled around my legs delightfully, with matching impossibly high heeled shoes. My silver clutch bag was on the table beside my tall glass of champagne. I shivered and tried to imagine what the champagne might taste like.

I was suddenly so engrossed in the fantasy that instead of being relieved when the music stopped allowing me to abandon the quickstep, I was almost disappointed.

Pierre appeared by our table and said directly to me, 'You do not have to dance every dance – you may sit out the next one if you wish,' so I obediently did so and sipped from the glass in front of me, watching other dancers, all of whom seemed totally at ease with the terrifying Quickstep. I leaned back and pretended to be completely at ease myself.

I so much wanted to become the kind of person who frequented places like The Embassy Club, arriving always in taxis, dressed so stylishly that others cast admiring glances towards me, a person who would never ever be embarrassed by a lack of social sophistication.

I reached for the little bowl of nuts in the centre of the table and tentatively tried one. It tasted exactly like a nut. I wondered what the little black things would taste like. Stella had said, 'Oh goody – olives!' and rubbed her hands together before putting one in her mouth. I noticed that she had then removed a stone or pip from her mouth and placed it back into the dish. It looked disgusting sitting there. However, I should do the same so I took a deep breath and took one, chewing on its rubbery saltiness in surprise. I could not bring myself to replace the stone into the dish so I abandoned it beneath the table and hoped nobody noticed.

Mr Farr dragged me from my seat for another Quickstep and told me that he had honestly thought I would be a better dancer and that in his opinion I had two left feet. I laughed and tried to look as if I was unconcerned, even content with criticism. Then, thankfully, it was time for the star of the evening, Miss Atwell, to perform.

We were told to applaud loudly at the end of each set and before I had time to wonder what that meant, I realised that all I had to do was copy what Olive and Stella were enthusiastically doing, and so I did.

Then, just when I was beginning to really enjoy myself, it was suddenly all over and the young man in dungarees was telling us that if we wanted to see ourselves on The Telly, we should make sure to watch next Saturday evening.

When I got home my mother was ready with the teapot at her elbow, eager to be told everything that happened, which was somehow irritating. I found I did not particularly want to discuss the experience because overall it had not been nearly as exciting as I had hoped. I wanted to lie in bed savouring the strange encounter with the other side of the TV screen and analyse it bit by bit. I suspected that quite the most enjoyable aspect of it would be casually mentioning it on the 8.10 to my travelling companions. I might even tell them that Guy really had dropped by halfway through the evening, on his way to the airport.

'I decided not to go to Prague after all,' I said a day or two later, waiting with Shirley on the platform.

She said that none of the girls had realised that he was a serious boyfriend and asked if I had a photo of him. I knew I really ought to try to locate something suitable.

A More Tactile Time

I had been in the employment of Francis, Day & Hunter for exactly ten months when I decided that the job was not providing enough stimulation and so it was time to move on. It was quite obvious that neither Stella nor Olive were about to give up a coveted position in the Professional Department any time soon and so there was no prospect whatsoever of me moving into that sphere. My one day a week on the switchboard was no longer providing the excitement it had initially and to be fair there are only so many celebrities who can be located by telephone within the space of a lunch break. The only reliable flutter of excitement on Thursdays was to book a table for two at The Ivy for Mr David Day and then to confirm that Miss Christina Foyle was available to accompany him. And of course Bob the office boy's broken jaw had long since healed and so I could not even look forward to the prospect of hand delivering something Very Important to a Superstar. I had one evening enlisted the rather unwilling Bob as a companion for the stake-out of the South London home of Tommy Steele, recently risen to fame via the Two Is Coffee Bar and still living in a terrace house somewhere south of the river. We spent a great deal of time trying to find

Bermondsey by bus because at the time there was no underground station nearby and then a great deal more, finding the modest little street. At least a dozen other curious celebrity hunters had got there before us and we were just in time to witness one of them giving a local child of about seven, sixpence to knock on the door of the new pop star's family home.

'Can Sandra come out to play?' we heard her say and an irate woman said no she certainly could not because she was in bed fast asleep. And shortly after that two policemen arrived on foot and gently moved us on. On the whole the idea had not provided much stimulus and so a change of working environment, if judiciously chosen, might do the trick.

Jobs were then very easy to find and so making a change did not pose any problem and in any case I had overheard in Julie's, the café at the end of Denmark Street, that Lawrence Wright, a rival publisher, was in need of a typist in his much acclaimed Light Music Department. I popped in there during my next lunch break and applied for the job. They hired me on the spot and to my great surprise were willing to pay me six pounds a week, a whole pound more than Francis, Day & Hunter.

I knew very little about Lawrence Wright except that he was spoken of in hushed tones because he was also the famous song writer, Horatio Nicholls and had written numbers like *Among My Souvenirs* and founded *Melody Maker* magazine. He had been born in Leicester in 1888 and his father was a violin teacher so from my point of view he had had a flying start as far as making progress in the Music Business was concerned. He left school at twelve to be apprenticed to a printer but the lure of the world of entertainment was very strong and so he soon ran off to join a concert party as a violinist and vocalist. However, by the time he was eighteen he had changed direction and decided to start his own business selling sheet music in the local Market Hall, ensuring good sales by singing the songs himself whilst playing on a rather ancient upright piano. By this time the talented young Mr Wright could also play banjo and mandolin and so he was able to augment his income in lean times by giving various instrumental lessons. He finally did well enough to open a shop in Leicester, soon establishing satellite shops in Hinckley, Nottingham and Loughborough. It was at this time he began to write his own songs and because they were turned down by London publishers he decided to found his own publishing company. You could say that by the time he was twenty one he was showing undoubted signs of becoming something of an entrepreneur.

He liked to tell his staff that he arrived at St. Pancras station on a wet and wild Wednesday morning in 1911 intending to see what London could offer him. Hiring a cart, he claimed to have pushed his stock of music and instruments to a basement that was to let at number eight Denmark Street, renting it for one pound a week. The pushing of the cart part of the story may or may not have been true but either way Lawrence Wright Music Publishing Company went on to gain greater momentum. When I went to work there in 1957, Mr Wright still arrived at the office each morning by taxi at eight fifteen am and as I was required to start at eight thirty my first job each morning was to make him a pot of tea and deliver it to him in his office on the first floor. He was infamous for some of the startling publicity stunts he devised such as hiring a plane from Imperial Airways in 1927 with the Jack Hylton Orchestra on board playing his latest number *Me & Jane In A Plane* as it circled over Blackpool Tower Ballroom then on to drop hundreds of copies of the sheet music onto crowded nearby beaches. On another occasion when publishing a number he was certain would become a hit, he bought the whole front page of *The Daily Mail* at the then unbelievable sum of one thousand, four hundred pounds, in order to publicise it. He was not known as 'The Grand Old Man of Tin Pan Alley' for nothing.

Mr Wright's large and imposing office was at the front of the building overlooking the street where he could conveniently keep his eye on everything that was happening below, which songwriters were entering which publishers, who was heading into Julie's Café for a cup of tea and an iced bun and who was proceeding directly to the pub on the far side of Charing Cross Road. I shared an office that would certainly have overlooked the back of the building had the tiny grilled windows been set low enough in the walls for us to look out. The woman I shared it with was called Delores and she seemed a very old lady to me at the time but she was probably only in her fifties. She lived in a top floor flatlet in Muswell Hill and had a cat called Jeremiah. I was typist to Mr Eddie Schubert who had fled Vienna in 1938 with his violin and found himself in London via a very circuitous route. Mr

Schubert was responsible for overseeing and promoting the company's 'Light Orchestral' music which included some of the stirring marches of John Philip Sousa of which I became very fond. The letters I typed on his behalf were to band leaders working Northern Circuits in places like the Tower Ballroom, Blackpool and also to BBC Home Service programme producers. Mr Schubert could be temperamental and had very fixed ideas about some topics about which he would lecture me at length such as the importance of keeping your teeth and gums healthy with a product called Gumtex which he assured me was a much better investment than toothpaste. I obediently bought some and used it and noted that it did not do for me what it obviously did for him.

Delores was shared by Mr Ted Raymond and Mr Joe Wisdom who were the senior song pluggers. Mr Raymond lived in a picturesque cottage in the village of Meopham, close to Gravesend, and he took a fast train home each evening from Victoria Station. Mr Wisdom on the other hand was a dedicated Londoner, originally from the East End but now resident in a Maida Vale mansion flat with wife and teenage daughter. On the ground floor of our building was the reception desk where a pretty Welsh girl called Olwen was both telephonist and receptionist and at the rear was the space where Benny and Lenny smoked and swore and sorted sheet music to be sent to various theatres and dance halls around the country. Benny was a tall and handsome nineteen-year-old with a motor bike and a girlfriend called Shirl and Lenny who had just left school, had thick glasses and pimples and got excited and sweaty when he spoke more than a word or two.

At the very top of the building Brian the Arranger and David the Copyist sat all day in an attic room, inscribing myriads of crotchets and quavers onto sheet after sheet of purpose-lined paper. Brian was to keep himself to himself for the duration of my period of employment but David on the other hand became something of a friend. At thirty-four years old he seemed extremely mature to me and I was flattered by his interest in me. He lived in Richmond with his unmarried sister, read widely and adventurously and was interested in Yoga. He had started his working life in a factory but somehow or other the fingers of his left hand had been sliced off by a piece of machinery and so, having played the piano as a child, and having a talent and interest in music, he decided to become a musical copyist. He told me that the accident, strangely, had been painless when it happened but that his foreman fainted when he saw the fingers on the factory floor.

With the new job I created a new and exciting imaginary family, venturing into the unfamiliar world of stepmothers. I was now an only child. My father, Joshua, a small town lawyer, had inadvisably married Jessica an actress after the death of my mother some years previously. I did not get on with her or either of her nineteen-year-old twin sons, who were called Brent and Stuart in honour of the Tarleton Twins in Margaret Mitchell's *Gone With The Wind*, and looking very much as they did in the film. Jessica had in fact auditioned for the part of Scarlet O'Hara but it went to Vivien Leigh and she never really got over the disappointment. Joshua realised he had made a mistake in marrying Jessica but had resigned himself to trying to make the marriage work. We had recently moved from our thatched cottage in Cobham village to a very new and exclusive apartment overlooking the river. My stepmother hated cooking and because help was very hard to find these days, we ate out on a regular basis at the steak bar in the Royal Clarendon Hotel which was fortunately close by or the new Chinese restaurant in the town centre.

'Your poor father,' Delores shook her head sympathetically and told me I should do everything in my power to be of emotional support to him.

'Do those twins have jobs?' she asked curiously. I had not considered whether I should make them work for a living but decided that Jessica most certainly would be opposed to the idea so I shook my head and said that neither of them seemed to be able to come to any decision as to what they really wanted to do in life.

'Your poor father,' she said again.

Life as a typist at Lawrence Wright's was immediately livelier than Francis, Day & Hunter and afforded me the delightful opportunity of meeting the rising stars of popular music on at least a couple of occasions each week though mostly, I have to admit, it was still only the would-be stars I was able to become friendly with. I was briefly enthralled by an actor who was toying with the idea of becoming a singer. His name was Peter Dolphin and he was astonishingly handsome. He was also astonishingly good at encouraging me to pay for every cup of coffee he took me out for and it only later became clear that he believed I might have some influence in the world of music simply because I typed in one of the offices. He did not believe in getting involved in relationships too quickly because he respected women. I thought that was rather charming because I was not used to being held in any kind of esteem. He was rapidly followed by an equally fetching actor/singer called Jess Conrad who again had a great deal of respect for me together with empty pockets when coffee shop bills had to be paid.

I was not being completely dismissed by the opposite sex, however. Not only did David of the lost fingers seem very anxious to walk me in darkened parks in the evening, and attempt to initiate me into sexual practices, but I soon found that Mr Wisdom also felt he had an obligation to familiarise me with some of the facts of life. Here was another man, this time a firmly married one, who was wont to expose himself to a teenage typist, albeit from the safety of behind his desk, shielded from more general view by an upright piano that he told me proudly had once belonged to Marie Lloyd. I tried to avoid being called into his office.

At the time men had far more licence in all matters to do with sex than they were destined to enjoy fifty years into the future. It was generally agreed that if women did not want to attract unwanted attention then they must take active steps to ensure they were not the recipients of same. A young girl who wore flamboyant colours for example, rather than adhering to safer beige and grey, was simply `asking for trouble' and those who accepted casual coffee invitations from the opposite sex ` deserved all they got'. Date rape was unheard of because if you went on a date and found yourself being raped as a consequence then it was very clearly your own fault. Reporting such a rape to the police might have resulted in the complainant being charged with wasting police time. A woman's place during the late nineteen fifties was primarily in the home, though with caution she could place herself within the confines of a hospital and serve the sick. Generally speaking young women looking for excitement got more than they bargained for. The rules were well defined and most people understood and accepted them. I was beginning to do so myself.

Had I been able to project myself half a century forward and observe cases of historical sexual abuse hitting the headlines in the first decades of the twenty first century, I would have been both astonished and fascinated. How could it be that a fifteen-year-old girl visiting a TV star's dressing room for fun, adventure and an autograph claim decades later that he touched her inappropriately? Has the world gone mad that now he stands in a court room, a sadly subdued octogenarian claiming no knowledge of the incident? What after all did she expect?

Furthermore those of us who experienced those unenlightened days of the nineteen fifties unquestionably have increasing sympathy for the melancholy procession of newly accused, challenged by fading memory and bitterly regretting the fun and games of yesteryear as they shuffle one after another into the courtrooms of the western world. And what of those more mundane and humdrum eighty- and ninety-year-olds now watching these cases unfold on multitudes of television screens across the world? Do they perhaps shiver a little as they unwillingly recall their own past stealthy and clandestine overtures to sulky nieces and uppity office juniors? Meanwhile their erstwhile victims consider vengeance. Like holocaust survivors pursuing concentration camp guards they carefully weigh up the possible emotional benefits of retribution.

'It was a more tactile time in the nineteen fifties....' One elderly accused says helplessly as he contemplates the evidence that builds like a medieval castle wall in his direction. But he might just as well say 'I was only following orders'.

In that more tactile time girls like me ran a daily gauntlet of minor mistreatment from males who pinched and prodded on crowded trains, emerging to onslaughts of whistles and loud and impertinent comments from males on the street.

'What a lovely pair love!' being the common observation I now remember as being directed most frequently towards me as I bounced along, desperately hoping my unhappy shape might go unnoticed.

Furthermore, in those happy days whilst men had license to be more demonstrative, on a whim more physically affectionate, women were restricted in ways that would now give rise to disbelief.

No Unaccompanied Ladies After 10pm – a sign displayed prominently in many cafes and coffee bars and one causing little criticism at the time because that was just the way things were. If you wanted to buy a cup of coffee at ten thirty and you had no husband, father or other male companion to accompany you then you would be wise to give up the idea and hurry home to a cup of instant instead.

None of these matters consumed me unduly, however. My own major concern at that time revolved around the Great British Class System and no matter how carelessly I created then discarded one family after another, at the end of the day I remained at the bottom of the heap. Not even a member of the Decent Working Class but somehow of an echelon beneath.

Sometimes on the fast train to Charing Cross, these matters were tentatively discussed between Ruby Benfield and myself. Now that I was required to start work earlier, we found ourselves on the same train. Ruby was a York Road neighbour and I had once been inadvisably encouraged by a cousin to send her an anonymous letter to 'pay her back' because she had passed the eleven plus examination and I had not. Unsurprisingly the letter had ensured that although we lived within doors of each other, Ruby had been directed to totally ignore me for a number of years. However all this changed when we left school at the same time to go to work in London.

'Them Benfields ain't so full of themselves now,' observed my mother, 'Not since their Ruby left the Grammar School and had to go and do a secretarial course.'

Whatever the reason, their Ruby was now allowed to have a guarded relationship with me. And we soon realised that we had some ideas and ambitions in common.

'I just wish,' she said on one bitterly cold morning as we stood together in the crowded corridor, 'That we could have an inside toilet at our place.' She said she really hated having to put on overcoat and scarf on cold nights before leaving the comfort of the kitchen fire to answer normal calls of nature.

I agreed with some enthusiasm and Ruby, encouraged, launched into a tirade against her working class family.

'I asked my Mum the other day if we could order some yoghurt from the milkman but she said no we couldn't yet she doesn't even know what yoghurt is. The milkman isn't too keen either because he said nobody else in our area wants it and it isn't worth his while to carry it – do you think your Mum will let you have it?'

I wasn't entirely sure what yoghurt was either so I just said I would ask and wait and see what happened. Ruby nodded and went on, 'She just doesn't seem to want to change and neither does my Dad. I don't understand why we have to live in York Road anyway. That house is really cold in winter and they won't do anything much to keep it warm. If me and my boyfriend Alan sit in the front room it's freezing cold in there but they say if we want to be warmer we've got to sit in the kitchen – with them if you don't mind. And my mum lets the budgie out to fly around the room and it does its business everywhere. And another thing, I'm thinking of dumping Alan you know because I really don't want him to find out that our toilet is outside the house. In his house it's inside, upstairs in the bathroom.'

She lowered her voice, looking around her before leaning closer to me. 'Do you know where I had to send him to go to the toilet last Saturday night?'

I shook my head and waited to be illuminated.

'Round to The Prince Albert, in Shepherd Street!'

'Didn't he think that was a bit odd? How did you explain it?'

Ruby sighed expressively, 'I just said it would be quicker...but you know I'm getting fed up with all these lies all about a toilet. I shouldn't have to lie should I?'

'How did you get him to believe it would be quicker?' I was grudgingly impressed.

She shrugged, 'Well he either does as he's told about it or I'll dump him – there's no way I can risk him finding out about our back yard lavvy.

And as these problems were enumerated I could only congratulate myself on the dumping of Barry. Unless he had a cast iron bladder I too, perish the thought, would be in the awful position of insisting that he pop round to The Prince Albert.

A comforting thought but even so the ever-present sensation of being alone and stranded on an island of inferiority and isolation did not go away and was made more intense on those Saturdays when I indulged in my favourite pastime, the exploration of London. I had been giving some attention to the City of London, that strangely insulated historic Square Mile that is placed somehow oddly apart from the aggressive commercial activity it generates. I read that somebody called Thomas de Quincey wrote *The Pleasures of Opium* wherein he talked of 'knotty problems of alleys, enigmatic entries and sphinx's riddles of streets without thoroughfares'. It sounded delightful and I couldn't wait to make a start. I might even read the book.

The astonishing tangle of alleyways and courtyards demanded the assistance of an A to Z purloined long term from the library and with its help I was dazzled to discover that indeed the heart of 'real' London still followed the original medieval street plan, giving the immediate impression of a city within a city that is best seen on foot because any mode of transport would of necessity simply pass by its most unanticipated hidden delights. Like Charlotte Bronte I soon realised that the visitor might find the West End pleasurable and amusing, but the City deeply exciting.

I began on a June morning at St. Paul's Station, soon discovering the site of the old Saracen's Head Inn where Wackford Squeers met Nicholas Nickleby. I found Ely Place, a private road belonging to the Crown and technically in the country of Cambridgeshire. Within, St Etheldreda's Church, the oldest place of Roman Catholic worship in London, was comfortingly familiar. I was the sole visitor.

I ached to casually order a gin and bitter lemon or even a Babycham, as advertised on television, at The Old Mitre pub in Ely Court but didn't dare to do so. If only my beloved Guy had not had to spend so many weeks away on that mysterious assignment! I purposefully walked inside, pretending to be looking for someone and walked out again, after looking at my watch. And in that brief call took note of the small dark rooms, the antique wooden tables and chairs and the stump of an ancient cherry tree around which the first Queen Elizabeth was said to have danced.

I wandered Hatton Gardens and discovered a passage leading to the only surviving building of Barnard's Inn, one of the Inns of Chancery. With mounting excitement I followed signs that promised to lead me to Dr Johnson's House in Gough Square, and so they did. And soon I found myself on Fleet Street, now at once recognizable and adjacent to The Strand, almost within calling distance of Charing Cross Station. These were the days when the street was still a bustling, busy place where, day and night it seemed, important-looking journalists in checked jackets some sporting red or yellow bow ties, stood in the doorways of pubs with pints in their hands, shouting at each other over the general din from the interior. The thrilling world of newspapers gave promise of being almost as intoxicating as that of popular music and I hankered to stand alongside one of these important people, sipping alcohol and hopefully looking elegant and slightly bored.

And briefly, with Guy still in distant Prague, the celebrated Duncan Webb appeared and immediately recognised me, waving a paper in my direction, 'How's Guy doing in Prague? Do come and have a noggin with me.'

'Thanks – I'd love a Babycham,' I said.

From the benefit of hindsight and half a century's distance I can now see very clearly that I would have done better to have thrown my lot in with the journalists and left the pop singers and their ilk in the lurch. At the time, however, the latter seemed infinitely more stylish and desirable.

The next time I ventured into the City area I explored the region east of St. Paul's, entering a maze of lanes, alleyways and passages, narrow thoroughfares that have somehow survived major rebuildings and giving the City its much talked-of charm. I made acquaintance with the Mansion House, the Monument and The Bank of England and the Halls of the Carpenters, Drapers, Mercers and Sadlers not to mention a number of City Churches and Britain's oldest synagogue, The Spanish & Portuguese. Coming across St Olave's Church I resolved not for the first time to acquaint myself with Pepys' diaries and subsequently did so, later setting out to find some of the places he spoke of on a daily basis such as where he ate his 'ordinaries'.

Sometimes I bought evil-tasting hot dogs from the street sellers that at that time encircled main line stations waiting to entice hungry travellers as they disembarked from weekend trains. At other times I ventured into coffee bars with Italian-sounding names and ordered cappuccinos and chose from the sweet delicacies of the time, pieces of rum baba or apple strudel both of which I came to erroneously associate with Italian cuisine.

On sunny days I walked through parks, Green Park, St. James' Park, Hyde Park and once or twice Kensington Gardens although at that stage I was still somewhat unfamiliar with places situated west of Park Lane and Marble Arch. And although I was still wildly excited to have become a part-time Londoner, someone who could confidently navigate the intricacies of the underground railway and to a certain extent the bus routes, I was at the same time acutely lonely because handsome Guy and others like him were merely figments of my imagination and there was nobody to share the excitement and the new experiences with. At the time I seemed unable to identify what the empty feeling was and would stand in front of those places that had most recently stirred me the most – the splendid Pillars of Hercules pub in Greek Street or the Theatre Royal, Drury Lane, and wonder why the electrifying delight was mixed with melancholy. I was at that time, unaware of states of 'depression' because those from the underbelly of the social heap did not suffer such troubles. Neither did they seem to suffer phobias or neuroses, leaning towards a more easily identifiable class of mental illness such as murderous rage where family members might be seriously harmed like that my paternal grandmother had visited upon her children. Straightforward madness that saw the children swiftly removed to the care of the Local Authority so she could be incarcerated for years, sometimes it was rumoured, in a padded cell.

My father had tracked his mother down in an asylum near Maidstone a few years after the war and we had visited her there occasionally on Sunday afternoons. At that time she had her most rewarding conversations with an insect she was convinced spoke to her on a daily basis. She stared at my brother and me without interest and no longer remembered who my father was.

As for my own state of mind, I was convinced that my quasi-emotional problems would be solved if I could become a full-time Londoner in a flat in a central area.

The problem was financing this dream on my limited income.

'I don't know why you want to actually *live* in London,' Ruby looked at me incredulously when I asked her somewhat half-heartedly if she would like to try sharing a flat with me.

'At least it would cut out this awful journey each day,' I tried to sound sensible but she still looked stunned.

'And in a flat at least we would have an inside toilet,' I was warming nicely to my theme now.

But Ruby said she would have the greatest of difficulty getting Alan to actually visit her at all if she lived in London. He didn't like trains. He even got motion sickness on a journey as brief as from Gravesend to Chatham.

In the nineteen fifties, towns like Gravesend lagged further and further behind the big cities. Door to door delivery services of one kind and another were not only common but still expected. Postal deliveries were made twice daily by a postman in a smart uniform who trudged the streets seemingly unhindered by his burden of mail. The coalman called once a week and had only recently upgraded from horse-drawn dray to lorry. Bread and milk still came each morning by horse and cart. Elderly males vied with each other over possession of the piles of horse manure that regularly soiled the streets, loitering behind carts and drays, garden spades in hand and eyeing each other antagonistically.

On a weekly basis the Rag and Bone man trawled the area with his donkey cart, initially handing over halfpennies for old clothes and odd bits of metal and later distributing goldfish instead but only if you provided your own jam jar. On Sunday afternoons the Winkles and Whelks man called between four and five pm with his pony cart and filled orders for pints of shellfish including shrimps for Sunday teas.

Sunday was still a day of rest for most people and at least half of the local population attended a church or chapel service of some description on a semi-regular basis. My mother managed to persuade me and my brother to attend more or less regularly until I left school and the desire to become a nun had taken its inevitable downhill descent. The problem with going to Church, I had always found, was that it was intrinsically boring once the dramatic effect of the Latin Mass wore off. She might have been more successful if she had been prepared to attend herself, but she was not and had always maintained that she hated the Catholic Church because of the way she and her siblings had been treated years before by a particular nun. The source of the ill treatment was most likely because the little Constants were apt to attend school on a most irregular basis because Old Nan had never been able to see any sense in it. In any event her daughters were more urgently needed for help with field work to boost the family income. It was inevitable that they would always be at odds with not only the Catholic education system but with the School Board Man himself. Sometimes The Board Man had toured the pea fields and hop gardens in his dark grey suit, polished shoes, navy raincoat and trilby hat with a sheaf of papers under his arm, intent upon tracking down miscreants. And then the tribes of truants had scattered as one, emerging from their hiding places beneath hedges and old tarpaulins only after he had safely returned to where his bicycle was propped by the farm gate.

And harking back to that time Old Nan said they were busy-bodies, poked their noses into other folk's business and they made her nerves bad. She'd been at the mercy of her nerves all her life she said, which of course we all knew was not true but she looked at us so intently and belligerently that we were silent.

Nellie half nodded agreement and poured more tea. It was Sunday and empty winkle shells were piled in neat little pyramids in front of our plates. We didn't always have a shellfish Sunday tea like many others in the street but on this occasion Nellie had been anxious to create a good impression with her mother because we had not seen her for a month or more and there was a great deal of family gossip to catch up on. As well as the winkles there was also a chocolate cake from Marks and Spencers the cutting of which Bernard was very much looking forward to.

I had been intending to broach the subject of flat sharing in London before the start of the new working week but as my grandmother showed no inclination to catch the five thirty bus back to Crayford I decided to postpone the discussion. Instead I took some sheets of typing paper and sat on the stairs with pencil and ruler, making a detailed plan of the top floor flat by the Thames, perhaps at Chelsea. I consulted the A-Z. Very possibly at Cheyne Walk. The walls throughout would be white, the furniture stripped pine and there would be plenty of bookshelves in the sitting room. There was a view over the river a bit like that from the wide apartment windows of my phantom family in Gravesend but not quite as extensive because after all this was London.

A Most Distinguished Visitor

Although I regularly bought the Evening Standard in order to study the accommodation to let columns it took much longer than I had anticipated to move completely away from Gravesend and Northfleet and into the long-anticipated London flat. For one thing it soon became clear that for financial reasons I would have to settle for something other than a flat. I might need to downsize to a room perhaps. Sometimes I spent an hour or so at the end of the working day touring the bedsitter land of Paddington and Bayswater and inspecting a range of dismal rooms. Sussex Gardens was a popular address for hundreds of typists and shop assistants who crammed themselves two to a room into the upper floors of once gracious houses, mid Victorian terraces of a style almost completely absent in Gravesend. When attempting to place my various extended families and their relatives in suitable housing in the area I had recently had to settle for the formal four storey terraces in Harmer Street, now impressively spruced up and all grade two listed. Fine architecture of the kind I would have preferred was getting harder and harder to find in the town centre. Several years previously, I had been oddly depressed as a thirteen year old in Coronation year to witness the demolition of a group of houses built in the eighteen thirties on the North side of New Road known as Overcliffe where I was reliably informed by my grandmother, all the toffs lived.

There had been lime burning there at one time she said, `And nightingales used to sing there of an evening – never mind all the palaver of them quarry men. The nightingales didn't fuss about them but just carried on singing.'

The houses on the other side of Overcliffe remained, and still do. They had deep gardens behind at that time, abruptly halted by the railway. The Gravesend Art School occupied three of them and I supposed that the remaining toffs lived in the others. I hoped so because occasionally I placed a relative there. In fact at the time I speak of my stepmother, Jessica had a sister living there who was headmistress of a large independent school a few miles away. Many years later, when living in Auckland on the other side of the world, I was interested to meet someone who had spent her childhood in one of these upmarket houses at the very time when I was purloining them for my illusory relatives.

The dwellings I now inspected in Sussex Gardens were on an even grander scale, once beautiful though now dilapidated. Built in the mid nineteenth century they had embraced all the modern conveniences of the age each boasting a huge bathroom somewhere above the first floor and two separate WCs one of which was in the basement. First floor balconies extended to form porticos stretching over the front doors and sometimes out over the steps to the pavement. Balustrades of ironwork lined the parapets linking each with its neighbour. It was all too easy to see how charming they had been just a century before.

But now the rooms were cold and uninspiring, furnished with heavy Victorian wardrobes and gigantic chests of drawers. Each room had a gas ring on which to heat soup, or for a more ingenious tenant to somehow make Spaghetti Bolognese or Chilli Con Carne. Washing facilities consisted of hand basins in the corner nearest to the door, installed in the 1920s when the places were last upgraded for multi-occupancy. Each room had a square gas fire set into the wall that needed to be fed with sixpenny pieces. Rent for a double room shared was usually about four pounds. I knew no other typist willing to share and so from time to time I met strangers who had advertised a wish for a congenial room-mate. None of them seemed terribly keen on me, however. Single rooms were more expensive and harder to come by. It seemed that whilst the occupants of double rooms moved on rapidly and regularly, their luckier compatriots with single rooms stayed put. One tired-looking typist from the Foreign Office told me she had never intended to take a room-mate but she had put her name down for one of the single rooms upstairs six months ago and had so far had no success in obtaining one.

The large sunny flat I had visualised in all its detail in the fifth form was rapidly receding and those schoolgirl dream days themselves seemed to be ten years in the past rather than two. Sitting in the hated maths class I had formed quite concrete ideas of a top floor in a leafy Bloomsbury square a convenient stone's throw from the

British Museum. I pictured myself wandering through the gardens to take coffee in the Museum each Sunday morning because although I had not read any Virginia Woolf, I had read a great deal about her and was in no doubt that she would have done similarly. In the back of my maths book on the conveniently squared pages, I had drawn a plan of this dwelling in patient detail and I was quite certain that could she be revived into life Virginia would undoubtedly approve. She would particularly have liked the access to the little roof garden I gave myself with its shrubs in various pots and cosy corners for curling up with notebook and pencil.

Later in that final school year I had cheerfully abandoned Bloomsbury in favour of an artist's studio in Chelsea. Needless to say I had very little idea as to what such accommodation was comprised of although I knew it was essential to have plenty of chipped cups in the kitchen so that I could enjoy drinking gin out of them with my visitors. Gin parties where the guests wore a range of outrageously colourful clothes and discussed art and books late into the night were going to be essential. I made the rooms in gin-sodden Chelsea much smaller than those of Bloomsbury largely out of ignorance of the true nature of an artist's studio. Later still Chelsea was dumped because my preference became Hampstead Village where I favoured a small attic apartment close to both the Heath and the tube station having little idea of the geography of either at the time. Once again, a plan of the accommodation was painstakingly drawn, this time on proper graph paper purloined from the cupboard in the art room. I even put furniture items into position in the rooms, at times with short descriptions regarding wood type, colour, etc.

Now, adjusting reluctantly to reality, I accepted the idea of a Bayswater bedsitting room. And until the right one turned up I lived a halfway existence, staying away from Gravesend as often and for as long as I could with the variety of new acquaintances I had cultivated from within the narrow confines of Denmark Street. And in this way I at least became familiar with a number of differing living spaces, in a range of suburbs, some very pleasant and some so hideous I was anxious to erase them from memory.

A secretarial friend from another publisher, Brenda from David Toff Music, did part time work for a well-known band leader who lived with his family in a rambling flat in a curious Art Nouveau style building close to Knightsbridge station. When he asked her to flat-sit while he was away on an extended working holiday in South Africa, she agreed, and asked me to join her. I was delighted. Later I was to realise that the Knightsbridge address was the most prestigious I was likely to have for a number of years. When Brenda went home to Pinner at weekends I took full charge of the flat. With great delight I invited Ruby and other school-friends for a Saturday morning coffee party where I served the 'real' percolator coffee I had found in one of the kitchen cupboards together with lemon cream biscuits from nearby Harrods Food Department. I had trawled the aisles in spellbound silence, turning my head from left to right in awe of the array of astonishing food items with price tags that hovered a mere fraction below their dazzling appearance.

Who were the beautiful people who could afford these foodstuffs? I made a swift purchase of the lemon creams and pretended for a moment that I was one of them.

The girls were impressed, first with the lift which was huge and intimidating, and then with the red and gold furnishings in the apartment, shabby though they were. And of course I did not say I was a mere visitor to the place myself but told them in an off-hand manner, that I had taken the lease for six months so that I did not always have to face the awful chore of going backwards and forwards to Gravesend night after night. The next weekend with Brenda again absent I inspected the contents of the wardrobes in some detail and tried on an assortment of the kind of clothes I wished I could afford to buy. Suitably attired I ventured back to Harrods Department Store and wandered the floors ecstatic that in Burberry trench-coat and brown calf shoulder bag, drenched in Chanel No 5 courtesy of my unknowingly generous hostess, I looked every inch a Sloane Ranger. Paying greater attention than ever to my accent and ensuring that not a single Kentish dialect word trip from my tongue, I tried on tweed suits and examined cashmere twin sets whilst bored but pleasantly distant saleswomen stood at a respectful distance.

It was difficult to relinquish the Knightsbridge life when the time came some weeks later. I had easily become accustomed to the weekend wearing of designer clothes and am now ashamed to admit that when I left, one of the much coveted calf shoulder bags left with me on long term loan together with half a bottle of French perfume. If their absence was ever noticed it was never commented upon.

Not all my short-term domiciles were of the Knightsbridge Art Nouveau ilk. I recall in shuddering and comprehensive detail the basement flat in Westbourne Park where I stayed for three weeks with Frank, who maintained he was Nigerian and most definitely not Jamaican. I never found out why the difference meant so much to him. The damp-proofing of the dingy little terrace house had failed and was evidenced on every wall. Cockroaches marched in battalions across the floor and what was reputed to be an army of rats thundered behind the crumbling brickwork. The house was crammed with immigrant families whose large numbers of small children sat on the stairs all day.

Frank was a member of a popular singing group and later it turned out that regardless of the details of his true ethnicity, what he had more importantly failed to be specific about was that he had a wife and children at his previous address in Kilburn. They turned up at nine am one Sunday morning, a large lady from Liverpool, her two-year-old son called Kelly and six-month-old daughter called Francis. Kelly had a confusing appearance for the son of someone hailing from either darkest Africa or the Caribbean, being very blond with bright blue eyes. Francis on the other hand was definitely of mixed parentage. Naturally enough there was a great deal of heated discussion when the unexpected visitors made their presence known and not surprisingly Mary, for that was her name, wanted to know who I was and where her husband had found me.

During the animated debate that followed, it became clear that when Kelly had been born and subsequently surprised his father with his appearance, Mary had explained to Frank that such a phenomenon was not unusual and that lots of black men had white babies. It was almost commonplace, she insisted, especially in some families. Frank, she told him, just happened to hail from one of those families.

'I came to believe you,' Frank said, 'and I gave Kelly my love.'

Then Francis was born and Frank began to wonder all over again. Why did Francis look like a mixed race baby when Kelly did not? He decided to move to Westbourne Park to think upon the matter and as he had met me in a publisher's office and knew I was looking for somewhere to live, he had asked if I would like to share his room which of course I did. There was nothing too unusual about this he explained to Mary. Lots of people in London shared rooms together.

Mary eventually agreed to have a cup of tea which Frank began to make whilst I went with sixpenny piece in hand to a milk machine of the type that once graced the corner of every bedsitter-land street in central London. Long disappeared, large blue and white dispensing machines, always referred to as 'the cow'. Meanwhile Frank and Mary argued. She cried and so did the baby. I sat quietly on the edge of the bed, sipped tea, and said nothing at all. Finally Mary was persuaded to leave and Frank gave Kelly a half-crown piece which he took and stared at without emotion, two -ear-old shoulders slightly drooping as though now quite resigned to being a white child in a black man's family.

'Why didn't you tell me you were married?' I asked when they had left

'I was going to tell you Baby, but I was waiting for the right time.'

'Did you really believe that Kelly was your son?'

'Yes,' he said, looking sheepish. 'You heard her. She told me things like that can happen between an African man and a white woman. I thought she was telling me the truth.'

There seemed little to say in the face of his gullibility.

'Of course things like that can happen but perhaps not as frequently as Mary seems to believe,' I ventured.

He looked slightly dazed. 'I gave Kelly my love – how can I take it back now?'

I had no words of advice to offer. The next morning I said I would find somewhere else to stay. I was not looking forward to a repeat visit from Frank's family.

'Are we still friends?' he asked.

I told him we were because I had become fond of him and definitely wanted to remain on his list of friends. He might even have served as a valid boyfriend despite the handicap of being black. It was due to his patience I had at long last lost my virginity. Apparently I had been hampered by the kind of hymen that preferred to remain intact. Lesser men than Frank had been known to give up altogether. I had even been going to tell Nellie and the aunts about him, mostly because he was almost but not quite famous and could be heard every Sunday evening on Luxembourg's *Top Of The Pops* and even appeared on television sometimes. Although we were still living through a time when it was almost but not quite shocking for 'nice' white girls to have relationships with black men, semi-celebrity went a long way towards toning down the burden of blackness. Anyhow I was not terribly nice and certainly not averse to being known as someone inclined to shock. I could almost hear Old Nan's horror emerging from the very roots of her scandalized pikey psyche, '...but he's as black as the bleeding ace of spades!' Now that poor Frank's marital problems had pursued him and curtailed our romance there was, rather unfortunately, never going to be a pressing need for any of them to know about him. I left the room in West London and wondered where I would go next.

Fortuitously a would-be song writer called Alan, who was decidedly white and whose last name escapes me, had inherited his parents' council flat on the violent break-up of their marriage. It was in one of the exciting new tower blocks, reaching towards the grey London skies, north of Euston Road. Alan said he had just broken up with his long-term girlfriend, Theresa. He was lonely and so quite rapidly became my new best friend. It was an odd relationship. Nevertheless for some months we lived together on a semi-regular basis on the eighteenth floor sharing expenses most of the time. He was a better cook than me, his forte being Spaghetti Bolognese and a variety of curries so he did most of the cooking whilst I made a sterling job of cleaning up the flat. It needed it as it did not appear that his mother had been anything but a most casual housekeeper. Living with Alan helped the intermittent aching emptiness that still assailed me and also aided with the self-esteem problem that did not seem to want to completely disappear. He was not a real boyfriend but he could reliably act the part when necessary and although he wasn't nearly as good looking, and much shorter than the now long-dumped Barry from my school days, he was definitely better than nothing and also he knew a great many people.

Together we forged a reasonably pleasant life for a few months, with Alan seemingly disinterested when I left to spend days or sometimes weeks with my mother and brother whom he never suggested he should meet. Nellie was of course still anxious to know what I was doing 'up in London' and preferably with whom. She had only grudgingly accepted my time in Knightsbridge and of course knew nothing of Frank and Mary. It seemed prudent to be more forthcoming now I had a more or less permanent place to stay if I wanted it. Nevertheless I told her only what I wanted her to know and after initially threatening to report me to both the police and the Probation Service, she at last gave in and began to boast to the neighbours that my important job made it necessary for me to live for weeks at a time 'up in London' at the expense of the company I worked for.

Again, boredom set in at Lawrence Wright Music and following the Knightsbridge sojourn I opted to join the workforce of David Toff Music a few yards along the road where I shared the front office with two song pluggers, a Londoner called Johnny Franks about whom I remember little and a South African called Hal Shaper who was some years later to become a prominent lyricist with a number of big hits under his belt. He told me about his romantic and interesting family. His mother had been from the Lodz ghetto and his father came originally from Manchester. He had trained as a lawyer, he said, but his ambition had always been to write songs. He was tall, blond and good-looking, very much like Guy, himself still languishing between Fleet Street and Prague and emerging only when necessary.

I told Hal about my own family, updating Jessica, the twins and my lawyer father, broadening some features of the group and pruning others. Realising I was now working alongside so many Jewish people, I decided to make an effort to show the flag and join them. There was a brief moment of both doubt and regret harking back to an incident in the third form when I spinelessly joined a small group of persecutors intent upon making the life of one Jaqueline Posner as unpleasant as possible.

'You're a dirty Jew,' Florence Fletcher almost spat the words from slightly misshapen lips that we had been told she was under no circumstances to be teased about because they were the result of something called 'A Hare Lip'.

Jacqueline Posner crouched in the corner and muttered something inaudible but her eyes wildly combed the changing room ever hopeful for brisk and bouncy Miss Finch the Games Mistress to appear.

Florence stepped closer into the corner and repeated that she was a dirty Jew whilst I moved in behind her and wondered idly what was so unacceptable about being a Jew and why Jewishness invariably seemed to make you dirty. We all knew that Our Lord had been Jewish after all. Or had he? Had the historians simply got that bit wrong?

'You're filthy like a sewer rat.' Florence was really enjoying herself and demanded of the three of us huddling uncertainly behind her, 'Isn't she?'

'Yes, she is,' we mumbled only a little half-heartedly.

'And you shouldn't be in our school – we don't want your type here.' Sally Carpenter, tall and slender, reached out a hand to push Jacqueline backwards so that her shoulders hit the wall behind her, then she looked towards Florence who nodded approval.

'You should get out of our school Jew Girl,' Florence stated with relish as the first tear began to spill from the victim's eyes.

'Come on girls, hurry up and change or you'll all be late for prayers.' The plump form of Miss Finch, red-haired and cheerful, loomed over us and we obediently began to disperse, Florence the first to head towards the chapel.

'Good girl Florence! – buck up girls, be like Florence'

'Miss Finch was Our Lord really Jewish do you think?' She looked slightly irritated and told me not to ask silly questions.'

'Why is it a silly question? I was wondering if somebody got that bit about Him wrong.'

'You have a habit of being impertinent,' she said for no very good reason.

'What does impertinent mean?'

'It's what you are being at the moment.' She turned and walked impatiently away.

It all seemed such a long time ago and now Hal Shaper listened with interest while I told him that my real mother who had died ten years previously had been Jewish. Borrowing heavily from Mr Eddie Schubert of Lawrence Wright Music, I added that she had escaped from Vienna in 1938 as a very young woman. Her name was Rosa and she had got work as a maid in the home of my father's parents though she had studied as a concert pianist in Austria. Theirs was a love story and his parents had not wanted them to marry, one of the reasons being her Jewishness. When they did he was disowned by his family and then tragically she died of consumption. He later married Jessica the actress, who was not Jewish and as the religion was not practised around me, I was unfamiliar with a lot of traditions, customs and rituals that I might well have been expected to know. I said that I was much better acquainted with Roman Catholicism, which was at least true. Hal listened with interest and compassion and said that if I ever felt I wanted to become more in touch with my Jewish side, he would be happy to advise. I thought that was very kind of him.

Mr Toff himself was an enigmatic man who said little. He shared the office at the back of the building with his secretary Brenda. One morning he announced as he carefully unwound his checked scarf and removed his hat, 'Today if all goes well we are to have a most distinguished visitor.'

Johnny, Hal and I all looked at him expectantly.

'At eleven o'clock,' he said slowly and deliberately, rubbing one hand against the other, 'Mr Charles Chaplin is coming for a meeting with me.'

Johnny and Hal said nothing and I said stupidly, 'Do you mean *the* Charles Chaplin – Charlie Chaplin?'

'That is precisely whom I mean.' He nodded and disappeared into his room.

We all exchanged eager glances and I worked impatiently waiting for eleven o'clock to arrive which it did of course but slowly. Nothing happened. At quarter past eleven Mr Toff emerged from his office and re-wound his scarf around his neck. He said to me, 'To ensure that Mr Chaplin does actually arrive, I shall now go out – I will be in Julie's and you are to come and fetch me immediately he gets here.'

He left. A minute or two passed and then an elderly man in a long black overcoat quietly entered the office, carefully and methodically making sure that the street door closed after him. He stood in front of my desk. It was undoubtedly the great Charlie Chaplin himself and he was much smaller than I had imagined he would be. He had astonishingly piercing blue eyes and silvery hair.

He smiled. 'I have come to see Mr David Toff my dear. The name's Chaplin. Will you tell him I'm here?'

I stumbled to my feet squeaking, 'I'll just go and get him Mr Chaplin, please take a seat.'

Both Hal and Johnny had also leapt from their desks and were vying with each other to comfortably seat this most illustrious visitor.

I was along the street and into the café in a flash, still squeaking.

My employer leaped to his feet. 'He's arrived?'

'Yes,' I said joyfully, 'and he's lovely.'

'Calm down,' he instructed moving rapidly from the café table to the narrow street outside. I felt like telling him to take his own advice but of course I didn't.

The great man and our boss conferred together for the best part of an hour and during that time I was called upon to make them tea, whereupon Brenda glared at me and said she would take it into them when it was ready. Hal wondered what the conference was about and Johnny told us knowledgeably that it was all to do with some background music for a movie. This may or may not have been true. When he left, Mr Chaplin nodded towards me, saying, 'Thank you so much for your help my dear.' I glowed for the rest of the day.

During my time with Toff Music Charlie Chaplin was the most notable visitor to the premises. I could barely wait to tell the members of my extended family which necessitated an unplanned two-day absence from Alan and the council flat. Nellie was quite enthralled reminiscing at length on all the Chaplin films she had been to see when she was a girl. Even Old Nan was grudgingly impressed saying, 'There'd be no side with him because he's just like one of us. South London he comes from. He used to sing in the pubs when he was just a little fella.'

She managed to make Charlie Chaplin sound almost like a neighbour though I knew she came from Stepney, north of the Thames.

My erstwhile schoolmates on the 8.10 were somewhat less spellbound and even Ruby said she found those old films really boring and not in any way funny. She couldn't for the life of her see what there was to laugh at.

My brief period of glory that followed the coffee meeting in the Knightsbridge flat was definitely waning and I was beginning to grow once again more distant from them. I could hardly wait to get back to the safety of the underground system and Tottenham Court Road tube station in particular.

Then, out of the blue, Alan told me that his friend Bill was moving in with us for a week or two until he found a place of his own. Bill was the manager of the Chas McDevitt Skiffle Group and operated out of an office opposite Julie's café, on the second floor above the Regent Recording Studios. The group needed a typist Alan told me and suggested that as it would be part time I should take the job on. I was more than keen to do so and two or three times each week once I finished at David Toff's office, crossed the road to my new workplace. I certainly enjoyed adding members of the fast growing Skiffle community of musicians to my list of 'famous people I have met'. They were relatively undemanding to work for, seemed astonished that I could so effortlessly produce neatly typewritten correspondence for them and in general demanded little from me other than I should go on doing so. This I was very happy to do as I was being paid a handsome 'part time rate' of ten shillings an hour which enabled me to earn an extra two or three pounds each week. This I spent on a multitude of bargain basement sweaters and skirts from the huge and wildly exciting C&A store at Marble Arch as well as on my newly-acquired habit of smoking cork-tipped menthol cigarettes. With a cigarette dangling from my fingers I felt at once more sophisticated and worldly and cork-tipped menthols were of course almost healthy. With the help of menthol laced nicotine I became better and better at being a hanger-on, appearing on the periphery of a group in Julie's Café at the end of the working day and quickly being absorbed into it, moving in and out of groups effortlessly and meeting would-be pop stars who all seemed to have names like Casey Chaos or Larry Lightning. And it seemed that everyone at some stage had letters or lyrics to be neatly typed up in triplicate, sometimes paying in hard cash and sometimes in a succession of cups of tea and bacon sandwiches.

'How about you coming over to Julie's this afternoon and doing some work for me,' suggested Morgan Jones, a Welsh pianist, a man of huge physical stature generally known as 'Thunderclap'.

'Me too,' added the small dark man who was always at his side, a song writer called Bill Crompton. He told me he was working on lyrics for a number he had great hopes for, all about a beetle from South America. Morgan and Bill were fixtures in Julie's Café at this particular stage, spending large parts of their day there, emerging sporadically to keep appointments with publishers. They were often still at the corner table when the ageing Greeks, Rene and Damos, current owners of the place, gave the plastic-topped tables a final wipe down at nine pm. Then Bill would nod towards Morgan and say, 'Bathhouse' before the pair of them headed towards the Turkish Baths just North of Oxford Street where apparently it was quite easy to pass the night cheaply. Years later I realised that Morgan was a particularly brilliant composer, arranger and pianist with a loyal and devoted following.

So I moved further and further from my former life in North Kent but still from time to time returned to catch up with the family gossip.

'You didn't turn up for June's wedding,' Nellie said accusingly when I arrived on one autumn Friday evening. June was Aunt Maud and Uncle George's daughter and they were very proud of her.

'Gone to Africa she has,' Nellie was triumphant, certain that I would be insanely jealous of someone who had travelled so far afield.

'Has she now?' I worked at sounding as indifferent as humanly possible though the place had possibilities. I had typed dozens of letters to Africa over the years and indeed met some quite interesting people who came from African towns with extraordinary names. I even recalled that back in the fourth form our class had been required to read a book called *Prester John* by John Buchan that had turned out to be quite diverting and even at the time made me wonder what Africa would be like.

'I had a letter from her the other day.' She rummaged through numerous papers on the mantelpiece and finally retrieved the letter in question from behind the clock.

'She's doing very well indeed out there – she says she even has a girl come in to do the ironing every Wednesday, just imagine that.'

'Can't she do her own ironing?'

'Course she can but she can also afford to have some girl, a black she is, come in and do it for her, that's the point isn't it? I mean when are you going to be in that position I wonder?'

I tried to picture the African girl who was now doing June's ironing and failed. Did I want a similar girl to do mine? I didn't think so. But my entire body bridled at her suggestion that I might.

My brother, then about eleven years old, chose that moment to come home, entering noisily through the scullery door and looking dishevelled. A single tear trickled down his cheek and he was out of breath, puffing and almost wheezing.

'Them bastards been chasing you again?' Nellie demanded.

He nodded and looked uncertainly at me.

'What bastards?'

My mother said nothing for a while and did what she always did when under pressure, poured tea. 'Boys from Shepherd Street make his life a misery – three of them – always at him – they never leave him alone. Frightened of them he is.'

'No, I'm not frightened,' he protested feebly.

'Who are they – what are their names?' For some reason the problems of the recently visualised African girl busily ironing for June seemed to urge me to put right the wrong being done to Bernard.

'One of them's called Gopal – I think he's Indian and he's the biggest.' Bernard's voice was unnaturally soft.

'Where are they now?' My own now unnecessarily loud.

He seemed to shrink back in his chair and he spoke ever more quietly, 'They're outside on Hinkley's corner.

And they were. Still swaggering under the lamp, chortling far too loudly and showing off to each other as you do when you are fourteen or fifteen. The biggest one, the Indian boy, had a cigarette dangling from his lower lip and was as tall as I was in my high heeled shoes.

'Are you Gopal?'

'Who wants to know?'

'Hey d'you wanna be Gopal's bird then?' one of the smaller ones, ginger haired, hands in the pockets of his jeans from the Woolworth's Variety Store hooted at the audacity of his own bravado.

'Yeah I'm Gopal,' admitted the boy who clearly was.

'I want you to leave my brother alone from now on.'

He guffawed and the other two snorted in unison.

'Who's gonna make me?'

'I am, that's who.'

He threw his shoulders back, enjoying himself, 'Oh yeah – you and who's army?'

I reached towards him, tipping the cigarette from his lip as I tightened my grip on his collar. 'If you dare to go anywhere near him again I'll not ask you nicely – I'll make you.'

His total surprise showed in his eyes together with something a little like a sudden pulse of fear. I pushed him towards the corner wall, thumping his head against it in harmony with my thudding heart 'Do you understand me you bullying bastard?'

'Get orf me!'

'Smack her one Gopal,' yelled the red-haired boy whilst the third offender retreated a yard or two, poised as if about to run.

I pulled the shoe from my right foot, for a brief moment regretting that it might be the last time I would ever wear it and turned my attention to the ginger boy. Somehow the heel became embedded in his cheek and he screamed half in excitement and half in pain, 'Get her Gopal – get her!'

I felt the Indian boy's fist land in the centre of my back and then my ferocious anger was unstoppable and engulfed every nerve of my body. I hurtled towards him and sank my teeth into his upper arm where his short sleeved shirt revealed light tan flesh. The taste of him was salty. The feel of him was unpleasantly gristly. He began to howl.

It was at that stage that Hinkley the garage proprietor emerged from his office.

'What the hell is going on here?'

'Stop her,' yelled the smallest boy. 'She's biting Gopal.'

'Are you hurt?' Hinkley was asking Gopal. I thought that quite odd. He should have been asking me.

'No,' lied Gopal, blood trickling down his arm. He looked at me incredulously. 'She's bleeding mad she is.'

'If any of you bastards ever have a go at my brother again I will slit your fucking throats.' I was incoherent with an all-consuming fury.

Now that Hinkley, very definitely adult, with the air of authority that comes from running a stable business about him, was safely holding onto the Indian boy, his ginger cohort said bravely, 'Yeah? You and who's army? You and who's army?'

Somehow or other it was the second shoe this time, slicing through the same cheek. He half sank beneath the lamp post, face growing pallid, bewildered.

'Hey, hey, hey…this won't do at all. This has got to stop!' Hinkley placed himself between me and the two remaining boys. The third one was now in full flight up York Road, heading for the corner where he could see the safety of home.

'These three are making my brother's life a misery – that's what's got to stop,' I hissed, now glad to halt and all at once overwhelmed with fatigue. My mouth was still filled with Gopal's blood.

Nellie was heading towards us, arms folded, followed by Bernard who tried to make himself as inconspicuous as possible, managing to look more like eight than eleven.

'Yes – those three are making my boy's life a misery alright,' agreed Nellie, 'And just look at the size of him compared with them.'

Hinkley looked at the size and nodded.

'And I just seen that long shadow of shit, 'she jerked her thumb in Gopal's direction, 'I just seen him punch my girl bold as brass – saw it with my own eyes.'

Gopal exhaled both doubtfully and noisily looking from my mother to his still bleeding arm and back again. 'What about what she done to me? What about that eh?'

'But she's a girl….just a young girl…' Nellie was clearly shocked.

'She's bleeding mad that's what she is,' repeated Gopal and for a second I thought he might cry.

I felt another energising surge of rage and lunged towards him again, 'And you'll know just how mad I am if you ever touch him again. I'll kill you.'

He stepped fearfully towards Hinkley who was in the middle of a sentence advising him sternly not to bully younger boys.

'You two had better go off home before I call the police about this,' the garage proprietor added, 'This kind of thing can't be tolerated.

The two miscreants as one decided to take his advice and sloped off into the darkness, trying not to hurry too obviously, to where the third still lurked at the corner of Shepherd Street.

'And you should watch your language,' Hinkley advised me. 'I've never in my life heard language like that coming from a young woman of your age. You should be ashamed.'

I toyed with the idea of hurling a further selection of my shameful language towards him in particular but decided against it.

'They shouldn't bully my brother. I'm just protecting him that's all. He's much younger than them and there are three of them. They should be ashamed of that.'

He looked at me with just a hint of admiration then turned his attention to Bernard. 'I don't think you'll have any further trouble from them but if you do come and see me and I'll have a word with Gopal myself. He can be a bit of a hooligan – but I think your big sister's seen them off.'

I retrieved my shoes from under the lamp post and we went back into the house. My ears were ringing and my heart still pumped with astonishing energy. I wondered if I was about to have a heart attack. Never before in my nearly eighteen years of life had I felt so much murderous anger towards other human beings. Had I been armed with a more effective weapon than teeth and shoes I would have cheerfully permanently disposed of the three of them. That awareness, though in many ways alarming, was strangely uplifting. Behind my barely-hidden lack of confidence and wads of low self-esteem there lurked a certain toughness and lack of fear and if I could have emulated a Gopal swagger I would have done so.

Bernard was looking at me with something like respect. We went back inside number twenty eight.

Nellie said she had coffee somewhere and found a bottle of Camp. It had an Indian on the label and I wondered if he might have been called Gopal. She opened a packet of Garibaldi biscuits that were being saved for a special occasion.

'My teeth hurt.' I was anxiously examining the heels of the new suede shoes, one of which was now decidedly loose.

Nellie said grimly, 'I bet them boys feel a bit sore too.'

Years later Bernard told me that by the following week the story of his violent and unpredictable sister who had beaten up Gopal and his mates single-handed had spread through the school population, burgeoning out of control and becoming extravagantly embroidered as it did so. By Friday there had been six thugs and the violence heaped upon them had necessitated at least two being taken by ambulance to the A&E department of the local hospital to have stiletto heels extricated from their bodies. More importantly Mr Hinkley had been correct in his prediction that he would not be bullied again which fact was probably due as much to his own timely intervention as to my own excessive aggression.

The Doppelganger Phenomena

By the end of nineteen fifty eight being a doubtful friend and associate of those who would be celebrities was beginning to pall. Typing letters for them, about them, about the music they performed was also waning in attraction and I longed for something more substantial. I began to envy those whose names appeared at the bottom of gossip columns in newspapers and magazines I read on my way to and from work, and often at my desk during times when the typing dried up. Why couldn't I be a writer? I saw myself as a young Marjorie Proops, hobnobbing with Godfrey Wynn perhaps and moving into journalism became more and more attractive. If only Guy of the racing green MG had been real he could have helped enormously. Imagine how impressed the family would be when they read my name at the bottom of column four on page six of the Daily Mirror. There would be no pen names for me. What was the point of all that hard work if I was not to be properly recognised? I wondered what the best starting point would be and took a book out of the library called *So You Want To Be A Journalist*. It suggested utilising local newspapers, writing letters-to-the-editor on subjects of community interest and submitting short articles of the same ilk. But what were the matters that might interest the local community of Northfleet and Gravesend I wondered. Ask around your friends, family and neighbours the book suggested.

'How could the community be improved as far as you're concerned,' I asked my mother one Sunday morning.

'What are you talking about?' she demanded tersely. She was doing what she often did on Sunday mornings in winter when there were few passers-by to observe this violation of the Sabbath; cleaning upstairs windows. It was a job that required intense concentration in order to maintain balance as the windows could only be effectively cleaned by perching perilously on the outside sill with nothing to hold onto except a bottle of Windolene and a handful of scrunched up newspaper. With her back to the street below Nellie now grimly but with a flair born of many years of practice, removed every speck of grime from the bottom half of the sash window before pushing it upwards with the hand that held the newspaper, and attacking the top half. I watched in admiration knowing that I would never be able to tackle such a task myself though nearly every woman in the street cleaned her upper windows in the same manner and had done so through decades.

'The Benfields have a window cleaner,' I said idly, 'Why don't we get a window cleaner?'

She retorted that the Benfields had a lot of things including a second hand Morris Minor on the street since August Bank Holiday so maybe they could afford the two bob now and again but she certainly could not.

The helpful how-to book had suggested that the writing of opinion pieces with a political bent, aided changes in society. Interviews should be carried out it seemed with the politically interested or active on your street especially around election time. I was not politically aware enough to know much about local council elections or even if something as momentous as a general election lurked in the immediate future and struggled to remember when the last one had been.

'If there was an election tomorrow who would you vote for?' I asked Mrs Newberry who now lived next door with her husband and two small girls. She was a tall, angular, nervous looking woman who hand washed clothes into the small hours and called it 'Dabbing out'. She sent her daughters, Janice and Barbara off to school each morning in freshly starched and ironed cotton dresses that were often changed during the lunch break for fresher ones. She nursed her right hand under one arm and said she was going to complain about the New White Tide powder because it gave her hands 'real gyp'. She thought long and hard.

'I've voted Labour twice now but each time the bloody Tories have got in so next time I don't think I'll vote at all,' she said.

'What kind of changes would you like to see for the average family?'

She was unhesitating, 'What I'd really appreciate would be a launderette nearby so my girls' clothes could be done more easier like.'

I was impressed. Who would have imagined that Anne Newberry would have any understanding of the existence of launderettes at all? After all I had only come across them myself in recent times close to Alan's Euston Road council flat.

Anne Newberry warmed to her theme, 'And if there wasn't the call for them like then I'd be really keen on some kind of grant, a subsidy if you like, so that the average family could have more access to the laundry. Though, they are hard on your clothes of course – and at the same time, they're dear…very dear.'

I began to be impressed. There was more to this woman than I had imagined, even if it mostly revolved around washing.

'Don't you think that would be viable under a Tory government?' I was trying to sound as socially well informed as possible.

'Well,' she leaned comfortably against the peeling paint of the front door of number 26 York Road, 'They never want to do much for us working people do they? All that lot are interested in is giving more to the toffs and the nobs. In America you know, every house has a washing machine! Plumbed into every house and flat they are. They have huge great blocks of flats there that they call apartments and each and every one of them has its own washing machine!' Her voice rose triumphantly.

It was clearly going to be difficult to get her away from her favourite topic.

'Have you always been a socialist?' I asked.

She lowered her voice, and leaned forward, 'My Ernie goes further than that – he's thinking of becoming a Commie.'

Old Mrs Foreman, edging out of her house to exercise Chang the Pekinese looked startled and pursed her lips disapprovingly as she called him to heel lest he be tainted by such a blatant mention of the dreaded Reds. I was somewhat taken aback myself because it simply wasn't done in the late nineteen fifties to be linked in any way to the ideas of Marx, Lenin or Trotsky. Anne Newberry looked at the dog critically as he moved slightly away from her doorway and said she needed to get some smalls on the line. She disappeared inside again.

Rather surprisingly, despite the general poverty of York Road and the immediate environs, even the British Labour Party had experienced occasional difficulty mustering support in the area, evidenced by the general march of ascendancy of the Tories who had already won two elections and were the following year to win a third. Even as a small child I had been a little bewildered by my father's dogged adherence to the Conservatives. I vividly recalled standing with him on the corner of the street to listen to the address of a young Labour candidate who was offering a great deal but being pitilessly heckled.

'Don't you want somebody to be on the side of the Working Man?' I queried, quoting, as we walked back down the street to number twenty eight.

'You don't want to believe what they tell you,' he told me firmly. 'The Working Man has got to stand on his own two feet.'

I can remember wondering just how sensible his attitude was given all the promises, pledges and guarantees I had just heard with my own nine-year-old ears from the Labour candidate. I knew that my best friend Milly's father never failed to vote Labour and she said rather vaguely that it was because they made sure beer was cheaper and gave free orange juice to children under five.

I asked Nellie what she thought of Communism and if she knew Charlie Newberry was considering joining The Party. She folded her arms across her chest and shook her upper body from side to side. 'I don't hold with it. You never know what they might do and you'd have no say in it at all because they never hold elections like we do so you can't have your say. They got rid of the Commies altogether in America and very sensible that was if you want my opinion.'

'Some of the ideas sound quite reasonable though when you think about it.' Though I knew little on the topic I persisted for some obscure reason. 'Things like sharing for instance.'

She considered for a moment before saying, 'Well if I was to be completely honest I would have to admit that there was never no trouble with Russia when old Joe Stalin was the Prime Minister. There was none of the argy-bargy there is now. The people must have really loved him you know.'

I reached the conclusion that politics was complicated and rather dull and therefore, long before the library book was due to be returned, I had more or less given up the idea of becoming a Political Correspondent. I would definitely veer towards being more of a gossip columnist, a sort of female Beverly Nichols maybe. And having made that decision I immediately felt more at ease.

I learned that Marilyn Levy, another Tin Pan Alley typist who seemed to flutter between music publishing offices almost as much as I did myself, had recently turned her attentions full time to journalism.

'I'm working at the *Melody Maker*,' she announced importantly one Monday morning when I came across her in Julie's Café. 'I went for a job there as a typist but the pay was so awful I told them I would only do it if they let me write for the paper and they agreed. The very first thing I wrote went into print!'

I was suitably impressed and wished I had thought of applying for a job at the *Melody Maker* myself. Thunderclap Jones, ensconced at the table in the farthest corner told me, 'Her Dad is a bit of a writer of course so she's got a natural talent for it I suppose.' He looked at me hard for a few seconds as though trying to assess if there was perhaps a modicum of that kind of talent lurking somewhere on my person and added, 'He's also a cab driver and he's writing a book about being a cabbie.'

Oh lucky, lucky Marilyn to have such a man for a father. Why was it that other quite ordinary-seeming people had fascinating, worthwhile relatives whilst I was stuck with my dreadful lot, truly the family from hell. I wondered briefly if my own father had he lived, would have risen to the same dizzy heights of creativity as Marilyn's. I considered the poems and stories he had in fact written to amuse me as a child, long since abandoned to distant memory, suddenly wishing I had kept them. Was the time right to resurrect him to some kind of established authorship in order to demonstrate that there might possibly be a similar dormant ability within myself?

'My father used to write too,' I said – adding honestly, 'He wrote for children....' But Thunderclap had lost interest and gone back to the musical score on the table in front of him absentmindedly murmuring, 'Well I suppose you will never know what you can do until you try.'

The first article I wrote was returned to me swiftly by the editor of *Fling* a newly established magazine for teenagers. The story was entitled, *I'm Not Mineo* and was about an Anglo-Indian dancer called Nelson Grostate who told me he was always being mistaken for Sal Mineo the American actor who had starred alongside James Dean in *Rebel Without A Cause*. I had met Nelson whilst hanging around the stage door of whatever theatre it was he was working at during the recent summer and we had struck up a half-hearted friendship. As a dancer, employed in the chorus on a regular basis he had impressed me more than I had impressed him. However, the editor was clearly not quite so easily captivated by chorus boys.

'...I know nothing of Sal Mineo and even less of Nelson Grostate,' she wrote, 'and I am happy to leave it that way. I am therefore returning your manuscript.'

In late 1958 I was clearly fascinated by the doppelganger phenomenon. My next piece was called *I'm Not Elvis* and concerned a would-be pop singer called Nicky Papas who assured me he was constantly being mistaken for Elvis Presley. Looking back I'm not altogether sure why I believed him because I could not see the resemblance myself. Once again the people at *Fling* were unmoved. I was obviously not destined to enjoy the same immediate journalistic success as Marilyn Levy. I would have to move further towards the more established figures in the entertainment business if I wanted my articles to be snapped up. I should have taken more advantage of the rich and famous I had brushed shoulders with previously. I now bitterly regretted not taking more notice of Jerry Lee Lewis when he had strolled down Denmark Street earlier in the year with his new and very nubile thirteen-year-old bride on his arm, days later featuring in most London Dailies. It even occurred to me that I might have judiciously conducted a lightning interview with Mr Charles Chaplin if Mr Toff had been agreeable.

The festive season was looming up again so the journalistic career could be temporarily put on hold. Decisions had to be made such as should I have a family Christmas in Thames-side Kent where I could harbour simmering discontent with regard to my relatives or should I throw myself on the mercy of one of my London acquaintances and share a bedsitter Christmas in Bloomsbury or Bayswater with Findus Frozen Chicken in White Wine Sauce. No-one I spoke with hopefully on the subject made any offer and so I opted for the former to Nellie's great delight.

She told me that Old Nan and several of the aunts would be visiting on Christmas Eve but we would spend Christmas Day 'at home' just the three of us and she had got her eye on a frozen turkey from the newly opened supermarket in Gravesend.

'Them supermarkets let you go round with your trolley just picking up stuff – you could put it under your coat quick as greased lightning if you wanted to. It cuts out all that queuing so it's a lot quicker to get all your errands done. And the poultry comes all ready for the oven – no more plucking and cleaning.' She sounded triumphant.

The plucking of the freshly-slaughtered bird invariably fell to her in years past, the act of slaughter to my father who could be relied upon to deftly wring its neck in the damp darkness of Christmas Eve, just before the Carol singers arrived on the corner of the street. Once or twice I had been allowed to try my hand at plucking but had been considered too slow to be effective.

On one dreadful occasion they had conspired together to execute Clarissa my pet hen of the previous six months and furthermore invent a highly implausible story about her leaping the back fence and flying away. But of course I had not believed a word of it and told them they were murderers. Looking at her limp and lifeless form on the scullery floor I all at once realised how much I had loved her. Clarissa of the bright red plumage, the graceful carriage and sweeping tail had been a Queen among hens with her white ear lobes and yellow shanks. How proudly she had displayed her freshly laid white tinted eggs. How fond and affectionate were her clucks and coos when she greeted me each morning.

Later in the night when she had been cleaned and plucked and lay ready to be stuffed with sage and onion, I crept downstairs when the house was quiet except for the disturbance of my father's snores. I kissed her now cold and chillingly unfamiliar corpse, and searched the pile of discarded feathers for a selection of the finest as a keepsake. I made her a promise that I would not eat a single morsel of her and I didn't.

'I've got my eye on a nice little plum pudding from the Co-op,' Nellie was saying, 'There ain't no sense in making them yerself these days. And I'll do a lovely white sauce with corn flour and milk.'

And so it was satisfactorily settled.

If I was going to be put under scrutiny for my lack of normality once again by Old Nan and her daughters an update to the wardrobe was necessary. I bought a loose black 'poodle' sweater from the Marks & Spencer store at Marble Arch, a trendy and voluminous garment in which pale faced models looked sensational. I looked like a bulky black sheep as I tripped across the station forecourt passing the Speak Your Weight machine in my new and uncomfortable winkle--picker shoes and forced my way into a space on the 6.40 express. I had taken to the reckless occasional purchase of *The Stage* to read on trains and in cafes in order to alert anyone who bothered to look in my direction that I was definitely not an average run of the mill shorthand typist but possibly an aspiring actress or playwright simply browsing the possibilities. After all had not the great John Osborne himself submitted his script for *Look Back In Anger* in response to an advertisement placed in 1956 by the soon to be launched Royal Court Theatre?

Christmas Eve fell mid-week that year. In the morning Nellie, accompanied by my reluctant brother detailed to carry the heaviest bags, ventured out to brave the bitter cold of Gravesend High Street to do last minute shopping. I could not be persuaded to go with them but stayed behind pretentiously examining the inner pages of *The Stage*. Milly Foreman from number thirty one and recently married called in to say hello and tell me how things were at Featherstones where she had just had a promotion.

'The only thing I don't like about being married,' she said, 'is living with Jon's relations. But we don't really have a choice because there's no room at my Mum's place.'

We exchanged gossip about this and that and I found myself envying her her newly married state. What bliss to be part of a proper joined at the hip 'couple'. Imagine the delight to have someone as good looking as Jon to show off to others.

'This is my husband,' I heard myself say to nobody in particular conjuring up Guy then abandoning him for someone called Jeremy who wore a Barbour jacket, drove a small, low vehicle possibly red and drank at The Six Bells in Cobham village or The Cricketers at Meopham. He was a country man, a farmer's son possibly. He had dark brooding eyes and his hair flopped across his face when he leaned forward. He was quiet, even with an air of menace; perhaps a little like Emily Bronte's Heathcliffe. I pictured myself as Catherine Earnshaw crossing the windswept moor with long strides to meet him, skirt billowing behind me.

'Do you ever go to the Six Bells in Cobham?' I asked Milly.

'Never,' she replied decisively, 'We don't go to many places out of Northfleet really. Our favourite pub is The Queen's Head on The Hill.'

At midday Nellie and Bernard emerged from the Gravesend bus telling me how you couldn't move inside the stores for the crowds of last minute shoppers and it was bitter cold out.

Bernard shivered obligingly. She told him his hands were as cold as a toad's back.

He studied them dispassionately as if they belonged to someone else.

'Do you remember that December you took me to the hospital?' he asked suddenly.

I shook my head, knowing exactly what he was talking about. 'What December was that?'

He looked nervously towards Nellie who seemed fully occupied stacking tins of baked beans and then back to me. In the aching silence we both contemplated the giant tusked hairy mammoth that was our dead father, always in the room at this time of year, observing, haunting, censorious. He had died suddenly and as far as we were concerned, inexplicably, shortly after being admitted to hospital in mid-December 1951 to make each Christmas that followed ominously significant.

'I cut my leg open on the Old Green bomb site,' he said at last, 'and Mum was at work. She said I was to stay inside because it was a really foggy day. But you locked me out.'

'I didn't lock you out.' But of course I did. I clearly remembered doing so, impatient to be rid of him.

Later it was called The Christmas of the Great Smog, now known to be the worst air-pollution event in the history of the United Kingdom. It was certainly the most significant in terms of public awareness of the relationship between air quality and health leading ultimately to the Clean Air Act of nineteen fifty six. It had started early in the month as an unassuming morning mist but thickened day by day, yellow in the mornings and stickily black by night. It settled relentlessly upon the town, hugging the strangely still waters of the Thames and lasting through one long week and into the next. Riverside towns were well acquainted with winter fogs that brought with them disruption to visibility and transport, that penetrated inside buildings and even prevented cinema goers from viewing the screens at The Majestic and The Regal. Somehow this one was different. It had taken us by surprise, creeping up on slippered feet seemingly just a run of the mill pea-souper, but ruthlessly stealing away health and vigour from both young and old. Day by day it became thicker, deeper, more treacherous until it reached into every corner of every home. By the eighth of December Government medical reports suggested that four thousand people had prematurely died and one hundred thousand more were sick because of the smog's effects on the human respiratory tract. More recent research suggests that the total number of fatalities was considerably higher.

The weather that had preceded the smog was bitterly cold and ensured that every household was burning more post-war low grade domestic coal than usual, creating the sulphur dioxide that aided the development of the event.

In those first days of December an anti-cyclone settled over the windless environs of the river all the way up to central London. Cold, stagnant air was trapped beneath a lid of warm air and so the yellow-black blanket stifling towns and villages became even more unwilling to move on. Within a day or two public transport ceased and with no disturbance to the air, visibility even in daytime was down to a metre. Somehow or other, though, Nellie shuffled her way to her cleaning job in Darnley Road for the Lovells because she was financially obliged to.

She instructed me that we, Bernard, aged five-and three-quarters and me aged twelve-and-a-half, were both to stay inside the house. As soon as she left I sent him outside to play with Hedley Davis and the youngest Smith boys within the murky gloom of the Old Green and firmly locked the door.

I was then undisturbed to read *Loretta In Love* the prohibited paperback on loan to my mother from Mrs Grace Bedford of Buckingham Road. Loretta, I later realised, was similar in many ways to Marquis de Sade's luckless heroine *Justine*. She was a thoroughly good girl who was always somehow or other falling victim to ill fortune. She was abused by all and sundry and her virginity had been cruelly ripped from her though she had fought tooth and nail to preserve it. That particular unhappy incident itself had been witnessed by a bemused servant girl returning to the house unexpectedly and powerless to help Loretta. I had just got up to the part where Loretta discovers she is pregnant with the evil Nigel Goodwin-Smyth's child. Although it is a child conceived out of rape she knows she must love and defend it. It was all very racy stuff for a twelve year old in nineteen fifty two.

'It's a tender little story,' Grace Bedford had said in a low voice, handing the book over cautiously and almost as though she would have preferred it to be in a plain brown wrapper.

Later in the week, sharing a pot of tea together she and Nellie discussed Loretta in a clandestine huddle in the Bedford kitchen, almost as if she was someone they knew.

'It kept me up late that book did,' Nellie acknowledged, 'It's not often I stay up after eleven reading.'

'But it's such a sad little story,' said Grace, 'I cried and cried when....' She looked uncertainly to where her daughter and I were totally engaged with the cutting out of teenage paper dolls together. 'When she's you know – with him like, when he takes her like he does.... He's a real bugger that Nigel isn't he?'

Nellie leaned forward, glanced towards the teenage doll miscellany herself and reassured that we really were wholly immersed, said breathlessly, 'What about when the scullery maid comes back.....what she *sees* when she comes back.... I've never read anything quite like that before.'

We listened carefully, concentrating on cutting, each in our own little bubble of intense attention, Joanne even humming a careless little tune. Not a word should be missed when adults were in discussion of that relating to sex, childbirth or divorce. It was then that I decided to push the book to the top of my reading list and tackle it at the earliest opportunity. I was able to make a start on it just as the Great Smog descended.

Bernard said, jogging me back to the present, 'I had been playing with Hedley Davis. I was frightened to come in and tell you because you'd locked me out while Mum was at work.'

'I'm sure I hadn't locked you out.' He was beginning to irritate me now.

'Yes you did – you were reading that book Mrs Bedford had given Mum that you weren't supposed to be reading.'

'Was I?' I tried to sound mystified.

The distressed voices had initially been muffled by the smog and I had even been able to ignore the urgent banging on the door for a moment or two. I now recalled only too vividly the antagonism immediately replaced with panic when finally forced to unlock the kitchen door and the frantic group of small boys tumbled inside. A human spiral encircled in an evil halo of yellow haze, they tried to explain how the accident had happened before disappearing with an unnatural obedience through the still open door.

A large part of his lower leg seemed to have split, exposing an inner expanse of pulsating purple, something that looked suspiciously like bone, and a great deal of blood. Feeling lightheaded and distinctly queasy I bound the offensive injury out of sight with a teacloth then pulled a pair of my dead father's work socks up over it one after the other.

In the moment or two when the door had been open, the tenacious pollution had seeped inside and now everything looked somehow insubstantial.

'Where are we going?' Bernard himself had become wraithlike and pale. He began to cry a little as I pulled him out of the house and towards the bus stop before abandoning the idea when one of the oldest Smith boys loomed up in front of me, leering - 'How many effs in busses?'

'What do you mean?'

'How many effs in busses – in the word busses? He repeated, his mouth open in an unpleasant sneer.

I wondered whether to answer but then said, 'There's no eff in busses' and he began to roar with laughter, delighted at my response. 'That's right there ain't no effing busses is there?'

'Piss off.'

'Who are you telling to piss off?' but he did so, suddenly bored with his own humour.

'We're going to the hospital,' I told Bernard firmly and began to head in that direction.

Not many people in the area actually owned cars in nineteen fifty two. No-one I knew of in York Road. We made very slow progress up Springhead Road and then came across an elderly man cleaning the windscreen of a Morris Minor.

I approached him as purposefully as possible. 'Could you drive us to the hospital please? My brother's had an accident.'

'I was going to drive over to my daughter's but I'm not sure I'm going to get there in this.' He gestured at the fog all around us.

I heard myself saying, 'Maybe you could try to take us some of the way.'

To his credit he agreed but said he had to go indoors to tell Phyllis first. Phyllis came out and looked at me in a hostile manner.

'She's one of those kiddies from York Road,' she said and asked me where my mother was. I said she was at work and I really needed to get to the hospital so that my brother's leg could be attended to.

After further consultation between them we set off, at snail's pace on what I now realise was potentially a very hazardous journey. Somehow or other we got to the hospital but it took a long time and Bernard bled through the tea-towel and my father's socks and onto the upholstery in the back seat.

The man asked if I wanted him to come in with me.

'That won't be necessary,' I said. 'And thank you very much for your help'

He said he might as well go on to his daughter's now as he was halfway there and he inched away wishing us luck. At least that's how I now remembered it.

The hospital was eerie and all the staff were indistinct, ghost people. We were several hours there and the injury needed a lot of stitches. In those days children had a great deal more autonomy than they do now and twelve-year-olds were considered of sufficient age and experience to routinely take care of and make decisions for younger siblings so despite the weather conditions no-one questioned why or how we had arrived without an adult. This was a time when a child as young as seven was, weather permitting, expected to be able to make journeys from one town to another on public transport completely alone. And although fiercely protected from all sexual knowledge that often extended to the details and mechanics of menstruation, girls as young as nine and ten took care of new babies, eleven-year-olds baby-sat for neighbours and sixteen-year-olds got married and had babies themselves. Our unaccompanied appearance at the A&E department would not have been in any way noteworthy.

Nellie arrived just as the leg dressing was complete, looking distraught and agitated. Somehow or other the news of both the accident and the commandeering of car and driver had reached her when she got home from work. She had walked the two miles from York Road. She swayed between castigating me for causing her so much anxiety and commending me for finding a solution to the transport problem. The woman in charge of the A&E department said we would be able to go home in the emergency ambulance because it was imminently about to attempt to make its way to Dover Road where an accident had occurred. They would drop us off there she said.

Nellie was very grateful and said that outside it was like being blind because you couldn't see a hand in front of you with this fog. She was sure it was going to go to her chest. Somehow or other we got home.

Now Bernard was staring directly at me. `When we got back from the hospital you were telling us a joke about how to spell buses - how many effs in buses,' he said, 'and I didn't understand it because I couldn't spell buses'.

'It wasn't a very funny joke,' I protested.

We were both recalling what details we could not of that December of the Great Smog but the preceding one when the abrupt death of our father shattered the emotional balance of our lives. Still under five, Bernard had been confused and thrust into watchfulness. He asked no questions, demanded no explanations. I felt relief at the death. No more father with his demands that I should perform better in school. No more father always in the background fighting with my mother, making her cry. Relief turning to simmering anger when days passed and no-one saw fit to tell me he had died. It seemed I should just quietly forget he had ever existed. Relief mingled with embarrassment when she at last chose to tell me but in front of a family audience. Old Nan, Cousin Margaret and a number of aunts all poised to note my reaction to the news as they sipped their tea and munched their ginger-nuts.

In the intervening years our now reduced family of three had spoken of him only rarely. He became the phantom in the corner, emerging into a gloomy substance every year just before the festive season around the anniversary of his departure when we acknowledged his presence to each other with small gestures but without words.

Just as the knock came at the front door heralding the visitors Bernard hissed at me, 'I don't always like Christmas very much.'

My grandmother was wearing her usual black skirt topped with a cheerful red blouse to acknowledge the time of year. In the last year or two the leg ulcer she had complained of for a decade had deteriorated and she had taken to using a stick, leaning heavily upon it when she wasn't jabbing it in the ribs of her younger grandchildren. Bernard, thinking he might come into that category now, placed himself on a stool in the furthest corner of the room.

She peered at him and remarked that he hadn't grown much then turned her attention to me.

'Well you don't get no thinner,' she remarked. 'You must be eating your poor mother out of house and home.'

'Not really,' I said sweetly, 'I don't live here all the time these days so....' But she had already forgotten me and was demanding tea and wondering if Nellie had managed to get any winkles in the town.

'I do love a few winkles with me bread and butter with a dash of vinegar, that's how I likes them best.'

And sure enough before she could complain further the sound of the shrimp and winkle man was heard across the Old Green and Bernard was dispatched for a pint each of winkles and whelks. The aunts sorted through their purses each pretending to be the one who was desperate to pay for them. Nan sat straight in her chair with a merciless, unyielding look on her face.

It was Maud who finally produced the necessary coins, having misjudged the half-hearted fumblings of the others. She handed the money over with the disapproving snuffle of the loser and a shake of her newly-permed head, shooting a look of pure venom towards her mother.

They spent the afternoon mercilessly tearing apart the reputations of family and neighbours and at opening time Bernard was sent to the off-licence for Guinness and later again for gin. Then, fortified, Old Nan sang several verses of *Dolly Grey* which as Bernard pointed out later, was hardly a festive song. The Salvation Army Silver Band trawled York Road, Shepherd Street and Buckingham Road and he and I went out three times to listen and soak up the atmosphere. By eight o'clock it was bitterly cold and thirty minutes later it hesitantly began to snow which sent Bernard into a delirium of delight. He was shivering, wearing his school blazer, too big for him and handed down from one of the cousins on my father's side of the family. He jogged up and down under the lamp post on the corner of Springhead Road, his head thrown back to better examine the sky. 'When I wake up tomorrow morning there's going to be snow thick like grass.' He looked at me uncertainly and added, 'It's not everything about Christmas I don't like you know.'

'I know,' I said and we went back into the house that was now almost cosy with a blazing coal fire in the kitchen grate. The visitors had not moved and were deep in a dispute concerning somebody's behaviour on a Christmas Eve some years previously.

'I wouldn't give her house room if she came knocking on my door and begging,' Old Nan waved her stick towards the fire, 'I always said she was a tight-fisted cow and I ain't changed me mind.'

'I never took to her neither,' said one of the aunts.

They had finished the gin and Nellie looked at the clock on the mantle-piece.

'Harold is fetching us later to take us back in his new motor,' Aunt Maggie explained looking a little anxiously at the clock herself.

It was nearly midnight when he turned up, rather worse the wear for drink himself and led a last sing song before piling them into the new motor and bearing them away in the direction of Iron Mill Lane, Crayford. We sat in front of the embers of the fire delaying the turning of Christmas Eve into Christmas Day by the act of going to bed.

The next morning we drank tea laced with whiskey before exchanging handkerchiefs, socks and bath salts, wrapped in holly and mistletoe paper. Nellie prepared the supermarket turkey and plum pudding from the Co-op which was consumed mid-afternoon together with little glasses of Cherry Brandy. I ate slowly and deliberately, speculating all the while on what would my ideal family be eating and drinking at this moment.

My fantasy mother of the moment was called Deborah, known as 'Debs' and in fact there was no reason why she should not look a little like Deborah Kerr. She was a widow and drove a lime green Citroen car. I knew very little about cars but my cousin Margaret's boss with whom she was having a closer and closer relationship, was the proud owner of a new lime green Citroen and I had been very impressed to see him give her a lift to her mother's house in it a few weeks previously. Debs the widow woman lived in a pseudo-Georgian house with four bedrooms and a huge bathroom on the new estate going up on the outskirts of Gravesend. There was a separate toilet downstairs by the front door adjacent to the smart little boot room where we kept our Wellington boots and the dog leads. Nobody's boyfriend was going to be sent out at night from this house searching for a place to urinate. There were two dogs, Afghan hounds called Boris and Bella. Bella was about to have a litter of puppies and we might even keep one of them. He would be called Sergei. We had a part time housekeeper called Annie who lived nearby and came in three times a week to do housework and prepare meals. The rest of the time Debs managed the cooking and we ate simple steaks with salad. If there was a dinner party, which there often was, Annie always came in to help.

Debs was the mother of four. There was a boy, Nick, slightly older than me (I was Toni again, short for Antoinette). He was up at Oxford studying history. Toni had decided not to go to university because she wanted to be an actress so was currently at RADA. Younger sister Sarah was sixteen and in her last year of school. She was going to go attend Sadler's Wells Ballet School when she left, and the baby of the family was Tim aged twelve and away at boarding school in Sussex a lot of the time. I shared a room with Sarah, the best room, overlooking the garden. There was heaps of storage space in our room but we fought a lot because Sarah maintained I was untidy.

There was a simply huge lounge downstairs called The Drawing Room by Debs with half a dozen leather armchairs. We had a dream kitchen of course with all mod cons and separate dining room where we ate dinner and sometimes lunch though we always had breakfast in the kitchen. There was even a small room quite close to the front door, near the boot room, that I hesitated about turning into a Morning Room. However, I did not really understand the function of a Morning Room so on a recent plan I had drawn of the house, I finally decided it would be The Library. Its shelves were lined with interesting looking, leather bound books of all shapes and sizes and there was a desk under the window where Debs wrote letters and I sometimes typed on a very smart, very new portable typewriter.

Debs ran a successful business as a dress designer and had shops not just in Gravesend but Rochester, Chatham and Gillingham as well. She had various lovers. One was a famous actor who looked rather like Clark Gable in *Gone With The Wind*. Another was a well-known writer of thrillers. I think the third was a minor member of the aristocracy. The one coming for Christmas was the actor and on Boxing Day we were going to watch one of his films on television. On Christmas Eve there was a supper party for friends and neighbours with Annie slaving away in the kitchen. After breakfast the following morning we sat around the huge tree in the Drawing Room and opened presents. I was given a leather coat, pearl earrings and Chanel No 5. Darling Debs managed the festive food mostly by herself bless her with just a bit of help from the actor wearing a striped apron and laughing a lot. Early on Christmas Eve they had gone to the market to get the goose and because it wasn't the first goose she had cooked, Debs turned out a simply splendid Dickensian meal. We drank red wine in slender glasses and the plum pudding was served with brandy butter rather than milk and corn-flour sauce.

'Have some more – it's got to be eaten up,' Nellie was hovering in front of me with the pudding remains and the pot of rapidly cooling corn-flour sauce at the ready.

'No thanks,' I reluctantly watched the candle lit table of Debs and her family recede into the far distance and instead observed Nellie heaping more pudding and sauce onto Bernard's plate before turning her attention to piling an unusually liberal quantity of coals onto our own Christmas fire.

Bernard, who had been Tim briefly back from boarding school only a moment before and regaling us with tales of how he did not really understand how he had managed to come first in Latin, was now completely immersed in demolishing what was on his plate.

He felt me watching him.

'One of the things I quite like about Christmas is all the special food,' he said. For the first time in a number of years I felt a strange tightening of my throat and an odd tenderness towards him, so much so that I was briefly unable to speak. He would have so liked the roast goose and plum pudding with brandy butter and I so very much wanted to give it to him.

I shrugged a huge and very bored shrug.

Problems Of A Technical Nature

There were a number of brand new resolutions to be made for the dawn of nineteen fifty nine. One of them concerned a diet which revolved around reduced carbohydrates and sugar and indeed, when examined carefully, very little food at all. That was the plan at least. Another involved writing articles about people who were already influential, famous or at least household names and not those simply aspiring to be mistaken for same. The only problem I envisaged was gaining entry into the presence of the exclusive few though in fact this turned out to be easier than I could have ever imagined.

My first celebrity of choice was American actor Hugh O'Brien whose name has now disappeared into the mists of those long forgotten. In the late nineteen fifties, however, he was a legendary figure and immediately recognised by all from seven to seventy just as long as they had a TV set, as the wonderful Sheriff Wyatt Earp. The series ran from 1955 until 1961 and it was almost impossible by the end of the last run to escape knowledge of his renowned personage. Indeed by the time Nellie acquired her first humble twelve inch screened set in 1957, his life and adventures quickly became her favourite show of the week and Bernard certainly agreed with her, placing Wyatt alongside Robert Horton and Ward Bond of *Wagon Train* on his list of must-be-watched. Later they were all to be knocked aside by the small screen advent of Ben Cartwright and his sons Adam and Hoss on their *Ponderosa* Ranch.

In January the Sheriff, in the form of the rather hunky and handsome Hugh O'Brien, was coming to London to appear in 'The Wyatt Earp Show' at The London Palladium. It was obvious and absolute that he should be my first victim. It was relatively easy to track him down because in those days he would either by staying at The Savoy or The Dorchester. It turned out to be The Dorchester on Park Lane, minimally less intimidating than The Savoy.

'Could you put me through to Mr Hugh O'Brien's room?' I queried with as much authority as I could manage with both clammy hands and very cold feet. The Savoy had already haughtily informed me that there was no-one of that name staying with them. The Dorchester asked no questions and within seconds it seemed I was actually speaking with Mr O'Brien's PA, a charming man called Clint who made an appointment for me to conduct my interview that very day at twelve noon. I was to present myself to Reception and Clint would come down and collect me. My first foray into the terrifying world of Real Celebrity interviews could not have been much easier and when I turned up with new notebook in leather bound folder, bought for the occasion one hour before in Selfridges, I felt almost like a genuine gossip columnist.

Hugh O'Brien was still eating his breakfast and he alluringly asked my permission to continue and offered coffee which I turned down. I sensibly decided I could not manage coffee with the finesse I would have liked whilst trying to control my trembling hands. I sat a few feet away and tried to look both business-like and slightly uninterested as I asked him a number of questions about his background, how he became an actor, and all the things I thought a real columnist might want to pass on to faithful readers . He told me I was 'kinda cute', ordered Clint to give me tickets for the opening night of the show the next day and said it had been a real pleasure meeting me. Walking up Park Lane later it was hard to believe it had really happened. Sitting in Forte's Coffee House slowly savouring slightly bitter coffee I wanted to shout to other customers, 'Hey look at me – here sits a gossip columnist who has just interviewed Wyatt Earp!'

I took my brother to the opening night and with me firmly propelling him forward we confidently walked through the pass door in the auditorium which I quickly learned was a more painless entry into the dressing rooms of the beautiful people than going into battle with stage door keepers. We barged our way into the presence of the man himself and he greeted me with a wonderfully familiar 'hiya honey 'and signed Bernard's autograph book. But best of all when I submitted the neatly typed one thousand word article to the editor of *Fling*, she did not on this occasion return it to me and I was able to see it in print with, miracle of miracles, my name on it. I invested in a dozen copies to casually drop before friends and family. Later I was sent a cheque for three pounds which came as a complete surprise because in my ecstasy of excitement it had not occurred to me that I would actually get paid for hobnobbing with the illustrious. In any event I did not have a bank account and knew very little about how to access one so the cheque was kept instead as a souvenir.

Over the next few months I inveigled my way into other hotel rooms and dressing rooms of London theatres, conducting interviews with stars both major and minor though sadly not all of my resulting write-ups went into print which in itself would have been discouraging had I not still been so thoroughly thrilled with what I was doing. One that was successfully published took place at eight one morning with an American writer called William Bast. The youth of Britain knew very little about him and generally speaking his name meant little to the average person. The only reason I wanted to meet and have dialogue with him was because he had once shared an apartment with the tragically and comparatively recently dead film actor, James Dean with whom I was posthumously in love. Apart from his book about the life he shared with Dean I had read nothing that William Bast had written but I desperately wanted to perhaps touch the hem of his garment and breathe the same air as one who had once breathed the same air as James Dean. He was staying in a little house in Derby Street, Mayfair and somehow or other I had by a series of manipulative moves, found the phone number and forced him out of bed very early one morning to see me.

'I only got to bed at four,' he complained, bleary eyed but opening the door anyway.

Naturally I was very careful not to mention the name of the one I so ardently adored and for forty minutes we talked about writing, his writing. He wrote scripts for television and he was very nice to me. This time I accepted a cup of coffee because by now I was becoming an old hand at interview subterfuge and no longer trembled violently when in the same hallowed space as the wise and wonderful. Later his agent, a rather more aggressive man than he, with an office in South Moulton Street, tracked me down and told me exactly what he thought of me which wasn't much.

Although I now described myself as a free-lance writer and even had cards printed to that effect which I liberally distributed to all and sundry, the writing was not resulting in any financial gain, particularly as I had still failed to master the mechanics of opening a bank account. No-one in my family had ever done such a thing. Most of the time they did not have any money that was not immediately spoken for and if they did then they sensibly kept it under the mattress.

My mother looked curiously at my small collection of souvenir cheques and said she thought if I was running a shop it might be a reasonable idea to have dealings with a bank but other than that she couldn't see the sense in it. She suggested asking for advice from my cousin Margaret. She now worked for a proper business man who was making a great deal of money selling tractors to countries in Eastern Europe and constantly complained that his success meant he paid far too much tax. Between the two of them Nellie was sure they would know something about bank accounts.

'You don't want to be going near no Bank Account,' my grandmother said in the grim tone of someone who didn't know what she was talking about but was determined to be heard nevertheless, 'I've never been near no Bank in me life – you can't trust them. Stands to reason.'

Some years later when Old Nan died on Christmas Eve nineteen sixty five, the cousin who found her also found several hundred pounds actually sewn into the soiled and stained mattress she had lain on for years that was about to be illicitly dumped late at night.

I decided to deal with the dilemma of uncashed cheques at a later date. After all the positive side of being a would-be journalist meant that I was now able to be friends with a number of 'real' writers such as Tom Merrin, a feature writer for the *Mirror* and Herbert Kretzmer of the *Sketch* who was pursuing twin careers as both a journalist and lyric writer. I had gone out of my way to court such friendships primarily because I admired their work but also because I realised that having associates, links and connections in the right areas could only be of benefit if I was to take journalism seriously. If I had known at the time that Kretzmer was going to progress to world fame as the lyricist for *Les Miserables* I would have been even more impressed with him and taken his friendship far more seriously but as it was that particular distinction was well into the future. From time to time each took me to those very places I had been too terrified to enter in the Francis, Day & Hunter days, such as the wonderful Punch Tavern and I learned to drink vodka and tonic which seemed sophisticated though I did not much care for it. It was Herbert Kretzmer who took me out for my first stylish and expensive lunch to celebrate a particular success of his, the details of which I have long forgotten.

'Let's go to Rules!' he suggested.

Of course I eagerly agreed and did not mention the number of times I had passed the place and fantasised about who had crossed the threshold over the decades. My eating out experiences to date were somewhat limited. As a child I had once eaten an exciting but uncomfortable meal of chicken and peach melba in a hotel dining room in Gravesend, courtesy of three women who had travelled miles to visit my father and who were always referred to later by my mother as 'them Greek tarts'. My only other experience of fine dining had been confined to wedding breakfasts of cold ham and salad followed by ice cream sundaes when various cousins got married, some of them at what were considered smart places. I did not count stuffed peppers and rum babas at Italian cafes in and around Charing Cross Road. Neither could I really count a three-course meal for three shillings and threepence I had once had with Ruby Benfield to celebrate her birthday before we boarded the home bound train. On that occasion I remember being very confused as to the cost and only ordered one of the possible three courses, just in case I had misunderstood and it ended up costing nine shillings and ninepence.

Rules with its wood panelling and wine velour upholstery, its linen cloths and heavy silver, not to mention its well-organised and efficient army of waiters, was terrifyingly upmarket. Herbert had clearly been there more than once before and addressed one of the tall immaculately attired waiters by his first name. This was definitely the life, I decided. Finally, at long last I was where I was meant to be. Fortunately for me my first notable dining experience featured a restaurant serving traditional English food with an almost totally understandable menu. The practice at the time was for fine dining to describe itself in French which was to confuse me on various occasions in the future, but not today.

I was able to glance through the menu hopefully looking like someone wholly at ease in this exclusive place and ask Herbert what he would recommend.

'Depends what you like, 'he said sensibly, 'But I always have the grouse pate, and today I might have the steak and kidney pudding because they are simply marvellous here.'

So I told him that sounded wonderful and I would have the same. Herbert said we should have a glass of red wine and I eagerly agreed, having never tried wine of any description before. I was not impressed with the taste which was marginally worse than the vodkas and tonics I had recently been accustomed to downing in Fleet Street but I certainly enjoyed the idea of me sitting there, toying with the glass and looking every inch the budding columnist.

We talked about our lives to date. He told me that he had been born in South Africa, one of several brothers in a Jewish immigrant family who had fled Lithuania early in the twentieth century. He had started writing for the Johannesburg *Sunday Express* and had been in London for several years.

I told him about Debs and her dress design business, about my two brothers and my sister, about the neo-Georgian house in Gravesend and my mother's lovers. He said she sounded 'quite a girl' and he would love to meet her. That, I thought to myself, is quite out of the question. I said it would be lovely for him to come down for lunch one weekend and reflected that it was a vague enough invitation and I could always invent a reason why it was not immediately possible should he attempt to pursue it. However, sitting across the table from him on that Wednesday lunch time I reflected a little unhappily that I would be forced to remember him for the rest of my life as the man who had first taken me to Rules and furthermore if I had not saddled myself with a totally invented background and family I might perhaps have got to know him better.

In the Spring I moved back in with Alan, less comfortably now because his girlfriend, Theresa had returned and there was talk of them actually getting married. And because Theresa was much more vigilant than Alan as far as rent collection was concerned, I abandoned my part-time typing jobs in Denmark Street and applied for a full-time secretarial job with Pye Records in Chandos Street, just north of Oxford Circus. They said they wanted someone who was at least twenty-three years old. I was soon to be nineteen but said I was soon to be twenty-five and once I had sat the required shorthand writing test carried out by a middle-aged woman called Madeline Hawkyard, was hired on the spot.

I was told that Pye Records had emerged in the middle of the nineteen fifties when Polygon Records was sold to Nixa Records. Apparently A&R man, Alan Freeman had been the prime initiator of the label together with pianist Joe 'Mr Piano' Henderson and Leslie Clarke, father of Petula who had been a child star in the late nineteen thirties and when I joined the staff was the label's most prominent recording artiste. Alan Freeman appeared to be the most senior of the three A&R men, a strange rather moody man in his early forties who lived with his mother but was on the point of taking a flat in Park West in Edgware Road. The other two Very Important People in our department were Mr Michael Barclay and Mr Philip Waddilove. Michael Barclay was thirtyish, blond and flamboyant and the senior secretary, Joan was in love with him. Philip Waddilove was also thirtyish, dark, less flamboyant but decidedly posh. He was, I was told, very well connected being friendly with people like Antony Armstrong Jones though at the time none of us knew he would soon marry Princess Margaret.

I would have enjoyed working for any one of the three but instead I was to be personal assistant to Mr Bob Rymer who represented the Pye International label. Mr Rymer was short and on the stout side with oily slicked-over hair and he looked a little like a door-to-door salesman. I was soon to discover that he kept sets of indecent photographs in his inner breast pocket which he liked to show to girls like me. However, despite his shortcomings, he at least had an office right next to the more dazzling trio of Freeman, Barclay and Waddilove in the basement of the rather charming mansion house. His function in the company was to encourage disc jockeys to play the International label's Golden Guinea discs, most of which seemed to feature dance bands from South America.

As most of the artistes themselves resolutely remained in South America his job did not bring either him or me into direct contact with any of them except from time to time by telephone. The more interesting performers like Joe Loss, Petula Clark and Lonnie Donegan headed firmly for the offices of Freeman, Barclay or Waddilove and sadly Joan was frighteningly efficient and needed no help in dealing with them.

Soon after I joined the company so did Tony Hatch from Mellin Music together with his secretary who was called Sandra. As I then shared the downstairs office space with her at least I had someone to talk to when the workload became low. Despite the irritation of being side-lined into the International label, there were occasionally some positive elements to the job, one of them being detailed from time to time to join Joan at recording sessions at Abbey Road Studios where we mostly chatted to Ian Levene the sound engineer and made cups of tea or instant coffee for various musicians. In retrospect I rather enjoyed the job at Pye. My desk was directly in line with the stairs down which everyone who visited our department had to descend and therefore I got the opportunity to meet and greet most of the visitors even if it was there that my contact with them ended. Furthermore Bob Rymer had a generous expense account and was not possessed of the kind of personality that made him the obvious first choice as a lunch companion.

You could say he was not particularly suited to the job he was trying to do. Therefore he invariably got to the end of the month without filling his quota of lunch dates and so we ate together from time to time at quite smart places. He could not be persuaded to try Rules, to which I was very anxious to make a return visit but we did try Quo Vadis in Dean Street once and were seen frequently on the top floor of Lyons' Corner House in Coventry Street which seemed where he felt most comfortable.

I had been introduced to the Corner House dining experience early on in my working life via the Restful Tray cafeteria in the basement of the Tottenham Court Road corner complex. I soon learned that as you progressed further up the buildings the restaurants grew grander, and had names like The Chicken Fayre, The Brasserie, The Star Grill and even The Flamenco Room. Corner House top floors offered genteel dining to those who hankered after it and there was at times even a quartet playing at lunchtime. The menu featured melon dressed with ginger, prawn cocktails, scampi, grilled sole and steak and chips. Once I had tried a prawn cocktail I quickly became a devotee and never having eaten a piece of fillet steak before I soon developed a taste for that too. Bob observed that I had a healthy appetite which I found rather humiliating and so explained in an off-hand manner that on the days when Annie did not come in to do the family cooking, Debs did not provide an evening meal. I had grown rather attached to having a Deborah Kerr look-alike as a mother. In fact I was fond of the whole family, so I talked about them frequently. When I talked about them to Bob he looked at me in a detached way as if he did not quite believe me which was another reason for not liking him very much.

I grew moderately friendly with Tony Hatch's Sandra and regaled her with stories about them, even inventing dramatic break-ups and reconciliations between Debs and her various lovers. Sandra said they sounded typically English middle class and she was glad she came from working class Jewish stock. Her parents were devoted to each other she said. I had by this time completely given up my Jewishness and I was thrilled to be put into what I saw as the correct class bracket. Old Nan, the Aunts, all the cousins, Nellie and even my brother could now be figuratively kicked deep into the gutters of the lowest strata of the working class and safely left there. I vaguely wondered how this could be managed if I came across the perfect man and we considered entering the happy state of matrimony. There would come a time when he might demand to be extended an invitation to meet Debs and my middle class siblings or whoever they may have been exchanged for in the interim. Perhaps a suitable family could be hired for the weekend and if not then it was probably best not to get too closely involved with anyone in the first place. Easy enough as I was still being largely ignored by most men and indeed the next one I would have liked to become involved with was very definitely married and the father of two small boys.

I met Doug Stanley one evening at an office in Dean Street, Soho, having been taken there by a disc jockey whose name I have long since forgotten who was single-mindedly searching for a job in pirate radio. He was keen to promote my secretarial skills hoping they might be useful to the station and should this be so perhaps at the same time curry a little favour. I had absolutely no knowledge as to what pirate radio was but I was about to find out because Doug, in whom I took an immediate interest, had recently been hired as a DJ for CNBC or the Commercial Neutral Broadcasting Company.

Radio Veronica, a Dutch offshore radio station had been broadcasting to Dutch listeners from a hulk in the North Sea for some years and by late 1959 already reached an audience of one and a half million listeners. It was owned by three brothers who I was told also ran a hosiery factory in Hilversum. Flushed with success they decided to try broadcasting to the South East of England and that was when CNBC was born and Doug along with Paul Hollingdale and a Canadian called John Michael came upon the scene and involved in the first English programming.

Disappointingly, it quickly became evident that Doug was unfortunately spoken for which was a great pity. The mother of the two sons was a territorial German wife. On the other hand the Technical Director of the station, Luuk Nijhof was definitely available. Later I found out that he, too, was married with a Dutch wife in The Hague but that knowledge was a bit into the future and in any event I had already decided to settle for him because he was decidedly interested in me and the novelty of that situation went directly to my head.

There followed an action-packed few months and being Luuk's consort of the moment definitely had its advantages. He divided his time sensibly between The Hague, where his wife lived, and London, where I lived.

He spent money quite liberally and, as Doug later noted, 'as if it was about to go out of fashion' and I found that very pleasant indeed. He told me he was thirty-four years old which sounded quite ancient at the time but he certainly looked a lot older and maybe he was because Doug also revealed that his wife in The Hague was fifty-three years old. Truth was not his strongest characteristic but I was more than prepared to overlook some of his faults. He stayed at smart hotels like The Dorchester and ate at stylish restaurants. He was very easily persuaded to dine at Rules. With Luuk I was not only able to return there on a number of occasions but also had the opportunity of trying The Ivy, Kettners, Overtons and Bentleys. Things were coming right at last. Not before time as far as I was concerned.

When Luuk decided that I should leave my job at Pye Records and work with him instead I agreed at once. We would have to spend time in Holland he said and he organised a passport for me once I had forged my mother's permission for me to hold one. I was still under the age of twenty-one but he did not seem unduly concerned about that. With him I boarded my very first airplane in great excitement and made the trip from London to Amsterdam in less than an hour, a feat that itself seemed quite extraordinary to me at the time. This, I decided, was definitely the life!

I was more than readily determined to fall in love with Amsterdam and for the first few hours in the city I could not get over the extraordinary excitement of being in a foreign country, marvelling at the concrete beneath my feet as we waited for a taxi at the airport. It wasn't just ordinary run-of-the-mill concrete. It was *Dutch* concrete! The taxi we rode in was not simply a taxi; it was a *Dutch* taxi! The miracle of it all was intoxicating. Luuk found my sense of wonder captivating. He took me for a long walk along the city's finest canals, a walk that stretched from afternoon into evening starting at the Dam Square and ending along the left bank of the Singel. I was enchanted with the gabled buildings, so completely different from anything I had ever seen in my life before, and wanted to explore every one. We went into a real *Dutch* café and drank *Dutch* coffee. Life could hardly get better.

We had booked into one of the city's smartest hotels and over the next few days he took me to museums and concerts. I admired Luuk's favourite painting, *Winter Landscape with Skaters* by a dumb painter called Hendrick Avercamp in the Rijksmuseum and listened to Beethoven at the Concertgebouw. Then he said he would take me to his favourite restaurant, The Five Flies, the interior of which was somewhat similar to my beloved Rules. A huge man called Nicolaas Kroese was the owner of the place and Luuk introduced him somewhat reverently, telling me he was a very important man and well known all over The Netherlands. Nicolaas was a charismatic character, talking with great enthusiasm on all kinds of subjects, his favourite appearing to be some form of numerology. I completely failed to understand the basics of the numerology conversation and after a while he and Luuk spoke together in Dutch. Whilst we were in the city we ate at the Five Flies very frequently and years later I realised that might have been because for some strange reason, Luuk did not seem to be required to pay for anything we ordered.

On my first visit I was completely overwhelmed by the antiquity and magnificence of the place. The restaurant was something of a museum and we ate sitting under original Rembrandt etchings and surrounded by antique Delft tiles and rare seventeenth century glassware and Luuk gave me a little lecture about the Impressionists of the Hague School and the atmospheric qualities of their landscape work which was a little dull. We stayed in the city for two weeks and although Luuk went to meetings from time to time with the men from the factory in Hilversum, I was not actually required to do any typing. By the time we left I had fallen in love with Holland and half in love with Luuk and it was sad to have to return to what I had begun to see as boring old London.

However, when we returned life was livened up when he invited me to live with him in a nice little apartment in Park Street, Mayfair, which also served as his personal home office and of course I agreed without hesitation. He explained that as far as my employment with Radio Veronica was concerned I would be his private secretary and would therefore not have to do any typing for Doug or Paul. I could not help thinking this was a pity because even though my head was beginning to be well and truly turned by Luuk, I was still more than anxious for a romantic encounter of some kind with Doug if at all possible despite his situation of being hampered by dependent family. I now realise that in all probability Luuk was concerned that as few of the other CNBC staff as possible should realise that I had joined the workforce because later there appeared to be considerable confusion about this.

As far as getting to know Doug was concerned, all was not completely lost Anyway because over the following weeks I was able to see quite a lot of him and admire him from short distances. Often a group of us would have dinner together across the road from the Dean Street office at the Angus Steak House, hardly Luuk's restaurant of choice but Doug and Paul seemed quite content with it and so, to be honest, was I. Invariably Doug would order a T-Bone steak and attack it ravenously with me watching admiringly and perhaps Luuk was not completely unaware of the attraction. On more than one occasion he would tell me later that 'Doug is a pig – he does not know how to behave. He eats like a pig those T-bone steaks.'

There did not seem a very great deal for me to do as Luuk's private secretary except to take telephone calls to and from the Hilversum brothers and manage a little typing. Technical problems were developing that I did not entirely understand. It transpired that the strength of the broadcast signals from the ship were not robust enough to penetrate the principal target area, South East England. A stronger, directed signal was needed and there was talk of getting a 5KW transmitter from RCA in America but it was going to take three months from order to installation and cost possibly fifteen thousand dollars and so the plan needed to change. Luuk insisted that he could build a transmitter as good as RCA's and much cheaper, in his workshop in The Hague. If the anxious

Dutch brothers provided the money he assured them it could be done within two or three weeks. In fact he would not even ask for the money up front; they could pay him once they were satisfied with his work.

'Darling we will need to go back to Holland,' he told me, 'so I can access my workshop in The Hague and sort out these setbacks with the transmitter.'

I was keen to be seen to take an intelligent interest.

'What kind of problems are they?'

He smiled and shook his head, 'They are problems of a technical nature my love – and I will easily find a solution.'

The brothers agreed and back we went to Holland, this time to a place called Zandvoort near The Hague where we stayed at a very pleasant hotel and ate each evening at a romantic restaurant on the windswept beach. And there, Luuk actually did pay for the food.

He left from time to time to attend to 'building the transmitter' and generally I was quite happy left to my own devices for a few hours. Sometimes at weekends we visited the ex-wife of Nicholaas Kroese. She ran her own restaurant at a place called Warmond, north of Leiden, and I seem to recall that although it bore little resemblance to its Amsterdam counterpart, it was also called The Five Flies. The place was charming in its own way because for much of the year a group of Hungarian gypsy musicians lived on the property and provided entertainment.

During this period Luuk had extended and intense conversations with both Nicolaas in Amsterdam and his ex-wife in Warmond about a matter that seemed to involve the restaurants and also the Amstel Brewery. He explained to me that the brewery had a controlling interest in the Amsterdam restaurant and that because of a business deal he had done in the past with Nicolaas Kroese, somehow or other the brewery owed him a lot of money. This may or may not have been true. I understood very little of what he was telling me but I do recall very well going to the brewery on several occasions with him and meeting men who had impressive offices and charming manners. Eventually the money he was owed was indeed returned to him in cash by the Amstel Brewery and in the light of what happened later it was more than possible that the whole story was one of his amazingly fruitful fabrications. Nevertheless it turned out to be a sizeable sum and we set about spending it with enthusiasm. Luuk took me to what he said was the Bond Street of Amsterdam and in the space of one delightful afternoon I became the stunned owner of two cashmere sweaters, a pleated tweed skirt, a full length soft, velvety suede coat, and matching shoes and handbag of the finest Italian leather. These items of clothing were of the type I had daydreamed about, loitering in front of Bond Street windows to admire and dressed myself in when hurrying to assignations with Guy at The Punch Tavern. I had not expected ownership to come my way so effortlessly, however. I at once fell a little further in love with Luuk Nijhof.

 When the transmitter was built, we were taken out to the ship where Luuk installed it and then met the Hilversum brothers in Amsterdam at our hotel in order to demonstrate its strength. Luuk switched on the radio in the room and Veronica's sound was magnificent. There were handshakes all round and the brothers now totally confident of the project, happily paid Luuk ten thousand dollars. Furthermore an extension of the lease on the London office was agreed together with an advertising campaign to attract potential advertisers to the new station. There was then heavy coverage in the major daily newspapers regarding the advent of commercial radio in the South East of England. I was exhilarated to be involved and part of it all.

'That bloody Radio Luxembourg will be shivering in its shoes,' Luuk told me, and added that even the BBC could not afford to ignore us.

It was when he was wondering if we should have a little holiday in Brussels or Bruges that it became clear that the transmitter was not quite as good as everyone had hoped.

'I am so sorry darling to have to put our holiday on hold,' he said, 'I was so much looking forward to showing Brussels to you but they are now telling me that the signal is interrupted and that there is a great deal of interference. I cannot understand what the bloody problem is. We need to go back to Amsterdam to sort it out'

So back we went. It was later explained to me in words of one syllable that the sound test demonstrated in Amsterdam had not been coming from the ship at all but via a direct feed deftly set up from a recorded tape in an adjacent hotel room. Later still I discovered that Luuk Nijhof was not actually a sound engineer but a heating engineer. It was all very confusing and hard to come to grips with.

We had just booked into a five-star newly-opened hotel close to the airport when the police arrived to arrest him and also to take me away for questioning. They did not seem to believe me when I assured them he was not a criminal and that I could only assume he had been framed for some reason. He maintained that Doug was behind it all. I found that hard to believe but rather naively I also found it hard to believe what I was being told about Luuk.

I was kept locked up for several days without being charged with anything and without being allowed access to the British Consul. Each day I was asked the same questions, usually by a different person, and my belongings were examined again and again. I sent up urgent prayers to God that the beautiful new clothes would not be taken from me. The men were not interested in clothes but on one occasion a rather aggressive female officer dangled my new handbag before me and demanded to know how I had come by it.

'Well I didn't steal it if that's what you mean,' I replied fearfully.

'Well who paid for this?' she wanted to know.

'I did,' I lied.

'Indeed? – and with what did you pay for it?'

'With money I brought with me from London of course.'

But the men who accompanied her were still uninterested and wanted to know more about the mechanics of what they called the embezzlement from the Hilversum brothers.

I sent a fervent thank you to God and repeated that I knew nothing of any embezzlement.

Eventually I was escorted to the airport to be put on a plane in the middle of the night.

'Am I being deported?' I asked.

'Yes, you are being deported,' one of the officers accompanying me agreed.

Being unfamiliar with the processes of deportation I accepted what I was told.

At four in the morning I was back in London, scarcely able to believe what had happened.

One of the first people I called upon was Doug Stanley packing up his belongings at the Dean Street office. He explained unambiguously how unpopular I was with Paul Hollingdale, John Michael, himself and anyone else involved with Radio Veronica.

'Do you realise what you've done?' he demanded, 'Veronica was the first pirate radio operation – if only you had helped Nijhof see the error of his ways instead of helping him spend money that didn't belong to him.'

'But I didn't know....' I protested tearfully.

'We were the first,' Doug looked gloomily through the grimy windows onto Dean Street below. 'We could have been great. Now other people are going to copy us....'

Indeed he was right because the format was rapidly copied and Radio Caroline was born. The plug was pulled on the Dean Street office without too much ceremony and following the massive publicity for the station and because of his involvement with the project, Doug was unable to get another job in radio for more than a year. I set aside any romantic ideas I still had about him with great reluctance.

'What will you do?' I asked a day or two later. We were sitting in a coffee bar in Old Compton Street and had shared a toasted sandwich. The delights of T-bone steaks at the Angus Steak House were no longer for us.

He gazed into the bottom of his cappuccino cup miserably. 'I've got a couple of kids to support. I might go back to welding.'

I looked at him more than a little shocked.

'Did you say welding?'

He pushed the cup aside, clearly irritated. 'Yes, welding – it's what people like me do when they have others dependent on them. It's called working.'

I wanted to tell him that he absolutely could not consider working as a welder. He was a disc jockey after all. His voice was destined to be beamed into homes all over London and the South-East. People like Doug did not do welding.

He was saying, 'It's all very well for girls like you who've got well-heeled families behind them to pick up the pieces – it's a bit different for the rest of us you know.'

Why, oh *why* did I have to tell him so much nonsense about Debs and the house with four bedrooms and the Afghan hounds?

I could almost hear Old Nan telling me I talked a lot of baloney and no good would ever come of it.

I lit a cork-tipped menthol and said, `I guess you're right – anyhow keep in touch. I've got to get home. My mother's having a dinner party tonight.`

Some years later when the whole business had almost been forgotten and Doug was safely working in radio once more, we did have an on-again off-again romantic involvement that meandered over a number of years and never developed sufficiently for too many negative incidents to cloud the pleasant memory.

It would be true to say that whenever I think back to the first few years of my working life, the sad pirate radio saga springs to mind very easily and has become somehow etched onto a London that was yet to become `swinging` and even seems to harbour an underlying core of innocence.

THE END

This story continued from
CHALK PITS AND CHERRY STONES
covering the author's earliest years.
Available from Amazon in print and on Smashwords as an ebook.

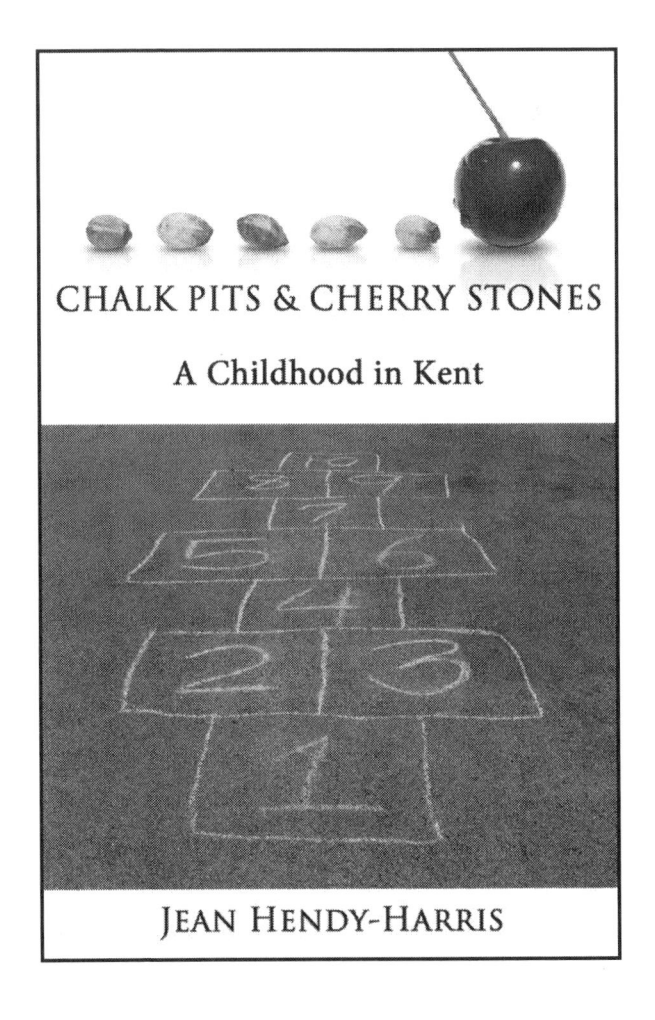

CHALK PITS & CHERRY STONES

A Childhood in Kent

JEAN HENDY-HARRIS

Printed by Amazon Italia Logistica S.r.l.
Torrazza Piemonte (TO), Italy